RAINER MARIA RILKE

Modern Literature Monographs

RAINER MARIA RILKE

Arnold Bauer

TRANSLATED BY URSULA LAMM

Frederick Ungar Publishing Co.
New York

Translated from the original German and published by
arrangement with Colloquium Verlag, Berlin

For the convenience of the reader, all titles are offered in German and English when the work is first mentioned in the text. For information about published translations, please see bibliography.

Though it is the rule rather than the exception that a poem does not survive conversion into another language, Rilke's language is frequently so private that translation of his poems presents special difficulties. For the reader who knows German, the verses that have been offered in translation in the text are given in the original German in a special appendix.

Contents

Chronology

1914–19: Lives in Munich
1916: January through June: serves in the military at the Bureau of War Archives in Vienna
1919: June 11: moves to Switzerland
1921–22: Rilke is provided with a residence—the Castle Muzot in the Rhone Valley—by the industrialist Werner Reinhart
1922: Finishes the *Duinese Elegies* and writes *Sonnets to Orpheus*. Writes "The Letter from a Young Workingman"
1925: January through August: lives in Paris. August: returns to Muzot
1926: December 29: Rilke dies in Val-Mont Sanatorium, near Montreux
1927: Rilke is buried in Raron, in the Swiss canton Valais. *The Windows: Ten Poems* is published in Paris

Introduction

Was Rainer Maria Rilke really the "last of the poets" as his admirers claim? If one connects a definite, traditional idea with the concept of poet, this absolute-sounding designation should, in fact, apply to Rilke; at least more so than to other poets of his time whose names are mentioned in the same breath.

What sets Rilke apart from Stefan George and Hugo von Hofmannsthal, the two men of his generation who are most often mentioned besides him, is a life style that is difficult to define. George was a German poet, rooted in German culture; Hofmannsthal was the prototype of an aristocratic Austrian. Rainer Maria Rilke never became integrated into society. He seems to have been outside of actual frames of reference, such as national affiliations and sedentary bourgeois existence. In his entire lifetime Rilke belonged to no group or clique, and he has had no disciples in the manner of Stefan George. Even for an artist or a writer there is such a thing as a middle-class career. Thomas Mann, who identified himself with the bour-

geoisie, demonstrated this by means of Goethe's life.
Rilke knew no home. He was a man without a country, one without financial security. He was a seeker
all his life. Restless wandering drove him through almost all of Europe, a nomad to the last. He cultivated
his loneliness in the midst of a steadily growing community of admirers, especially devoted women who
were ready to serve him. His life of aristocratic va-
grancy seems antiquated, almost archaic.

This portrayal of Rilke does not strive to add
another explanation to the many interpretations of his
work. It is an attempt to understand his life through
the eyes of our time. The phenomenon of Rilke's work
and mode of existence will pose a puzzle for each
new generation, raising questions that have hitherto
not been fully answered. The Orphic character of
Rilke's later work especially is still hardly accessible,
despite advances in semantics and psychoanalysis. The
fame of his name has endowed him with a certain
mystique. Rilke was even regarded with pseudoreli-
gious adoration. His fame, however, was and is subject to fluctuations. From the adoring enthusiasm of
those in the Youth Movement during World War I,
through the years thereafter and into our day, Rainer
Maria Rilke's star—now brighter, now dimmer—has
hardly waned. His is the world fame of a German
poet who, one should remember, is quoted abroad
more often than any other German lyric poet since
Goethe and Heine. The name Rilke appears in the
memoirs of many distinguished Europeans. In France,
André Gide and Paul Valéry are among those who

extolled him. In Russia, Boris Pasternak and Ilya Ehrenburg honored his memory with sincere warmth. In the United States, Herbert Marcuse, the psychologizing philosopher, sees in Rilke a spirit who freed imagination "beyond repressive tolerance" by combining within himself Orpheus and Narcissus.

1

*Poets
in the Old
Austrian
Empire*

The city of Prague, where Rainer Maria Rilke was born on December 4, 1875, had, in the second half of the last century, kept its exterior beauty: the architectural silhouette of Karl IV's historical Imperial City. But this framework no longer corresponded to the situation that then existed. The German ruling class felt threatened by the Czechoslovakian drive toward independence. To the Czech people Prague was already "their" capital. The Czechoslovakian part of the population grew steadily; the German part decreased. Of two hundred thousand inhabitants in 1880, only one-fifth spoke German. The Czechs had won their spiritual autonomy; they had their own schools, academies, theaters, and museums. Still, the German citizenry of Prague tried to maintain their superiority, an undertaking possibly made more difficult by the fact that its ranks were divided by strife. The German-speaking Jews—who formed an important part of the culture—stood between the nationalities. The German bourgoisie looked toward Vienna, as opposed to the Germans in the Bohemian border regions, who thought in terms of a "Greater Germany" and looked up to the German Reich. Rilke's parents belonged to that segment of Prague's population that was faithful to Hapsburg imperialism and was liberal enough to want to live in peaceful association with the Czechs.

These liberal Austrians, in friendly neighborliness with their Jewish compatriots, made up the intellectual countenance of the cultural province that was Prague. The first literary encouragement for the young Rainer Maria Rilke came from these circles. The feuilleton editor Alfred Klaar—who later went to Berlin to work on the *Vossische Zeitung*—and Hugo Salus, a lyric poet of Prague, were the earliest supporters of his young talent. The literary climate of Prague was to a great extent determined by these two writers; it was a climate of moderation. Only after 1910 did Prague experience a bloom in literature, as the names of Kafka, Werfel, and Max Brod indicate. But by this time, the young Rilke had long since left the city.

Even though Rilke thought as a cosmopolite from his youth, he always remained well aware of his origins. The Bohemian-Slavic element was familiar to him since childhood, and even though he never quite mastered the Czech language, traces of it continued to reveal themselves in his later works. As a young man he loved the intonation of the Slavic languages, the musicality of the Bohemian tongue. But that was just about the only thing that bound him to the old Austrian Empire.

The philosopher Rudolf Kassner, a friend of Rilke's who knew his works well, emphasized that Rilke had a "less than happy relationship to Austria," notwithstanding his *Weise von Liebe und Tod des Cornets Christoph Rilke* (The Lay of the Love and Death of Cornet Christopher Rilke), which is sometimes interpreted as being patriotic. Kassner attributes Rilke's less than happy relationship to Austria to the climate of his parent's conflict-ridden home. Rilke's father, Josef Rilke, was a former sergeant who had aspired to an officer's commission in the imperial army. He had advanced no further than the post of a minor

railroad official—stationmaster and, later, cashier—
and even this was due solely to the influence of his
brother, Jaroslaw Rilke. Rilke's mother, Sophia, called
Phia, the daughter of an imperial counsellor Entz,
came from an old Prague family. The child was chris-
tened René Maria. Like many parents, the Rilkes
wanted their son to achieve what had been denied
his father. René was to become an officer. This was
most of all the wish of his mother, whose fantasies
used to dwell in exalted regions. Phia Rilke's plans
for her son were rather foolish because it became apparent rather early that the boy's constitution was ex-
ceedingly delicate and that he was at the same time
of extreme sensitivity. A reason for this may have been
the fact that René was a seven-month infant. In any
case, the educational guidelines his parents followed
were full of contradictions, since they pampered little
René, let alone subjecting him to militarylike severity.

Up to René's sixth year, Phia Rilke raised her
small son as if he were a girl and dressed him accord-
ingly. His preferred toys were dolls. As his mother
told it, she could never get over the fact of having
given birth to a son. Her beloved first child had been
a daughter who died in infancy.

It can safely be assumed that Rilke's mother was
unstable to the point of mental illness. She was a
bigoted hypocrite, without religious depth, and she
had assumed a role quite fashionable at the turn of
the century: that of the misunderstood wife. Her marriage to Josef Rilke, an imposing-looking man with a
full and well-groomed beard, was not harmonious; it

was her belief that she had married beneath her social status. On the other hand, Josef Rilke was not the domestic tyrant one might have imagined a former sergeant to be, but a man tenderly solicitous of his wife and child. Rilke had no trouble in maintaining a childlike affection for his father, who was a far simpler person than his difficult mother.

Phia Rilke was quite gifted artistically, but to her son she was anything but a model he cared to emulate. Through his lifetime Rilke's relationship to his mother wavered between tenderness and rejection. He felt her exaggerated worry and loving care to be a burden. With the passing years the estrangement grew, and the poet once confessed, rather irritated: "I am no good at love, because I did not love my mother." Decades later, the inner chasm between mother and son still vibrates in the lines of his poems:

> Ah, woe is me, my mother rends me.
> Then I put stone upon stone around me
> And stood there like a little house,
> Around which day moved magnificently,
> Even alone.
> Now comes my mother, comes and rends me.[1]

The psychological analysis of a personality is one thing, the interpretation of a work something else again. Rilke himself resolutely resisted psychotherapy when his motherly friend, the writer and amateur-psychotherapist Lou Andreas-Salomé, once suggested it to him. Despite this, he expressed on several occasions a positive opinion about the theories of depth psychology, especially about the teachings of Freud.

He himself, however, wanted to be spared. As he once wrote to Lou, the thought of "bringing up his childhood piecemeal" filled him with terror. He wanted to transform the "unconquered" into poetry, into "things invented and things felt."

No less relevant to the development of the young poetic talent are important factors outside the psychological realm: the place the poet occupies in society, his bourgeois career, or at least his try at one. The image in which Rilke's parents raised their son was aristocratic rather than middle class, because the Rilkes had convinced themselves they were of aristocratic lineage. The entire family nurtured this fantasy of nobility. Yet only Rilke's uncle Jaroslaw managed to be knighted, for his distinguished service as notary and delegate to the Bohemian Diet. The Rilkes' ambition to be on a par with nobility may also have been the immediate reason for putting the delicate René into the rough custody of a military school. After the first years spent in an educational establishment run by a clerical order in Prague, the little René Rilke, barely eleven years old, entered the military school in Sankt Pölten (Lower Austria) . At fifteen, he managed to reach the next higher step in the career that had been chosen for him: the military high school in Mährisch-Weißkirchen. This, however, he could bear for only a few more months.

Reflecting upon this experience in later years, Rilke condemned his military education as "the dungeon of childhood." In a letter to a former teacher, he even likened the military high school to Dostoyevski's *House of the Dead*. Severity, the immutable principle of a military education, also determined the so-called comradery, which, in an exceptional case, encompassed self-administered justice. Although *Die Aufzeichnungen des Malte Laurids Brigge* (The Notebooks of Malte Laurids Brigge) can be viewed as autobiographical only in a very limited sense, the following passage obviously refers to Rilke's experiences at the military school: "When I was a boy, they slapped my face and said I was a coward. That was, because my fear was not the right one. But since then, I have learned to fear with that true fear that only grows when the strength grows that creates it."

The methods used in a military school in the Austrian Empire were, however, relatively mild compared to the ones employed in the Prussia of those days. At least René was allowed to write poems and even recite them in class. Although some of his classmates may have been awed by it, this display of his early emerging talent was an added incentive to chide him for "girlish softness" and to taunt and tease him. Yet one need not imagine the years of Rilke's childhood as pure martyrdom. He did not lack friends, at least not people who already felt the magic in his words. In this way he managed to ward off many a foe, and is even said to have been able to calm vicious dogs.

There may also have been something attractive to René in the military, if only the elegant dress uniform. Old photographs show him in a quite deliberate, slightly foppish pose. It is possible that René, too, saw himself as "cornet."

There is hardly any doubt that Rilke also be-

lieved in his noble descent. More certain than anyone
was the community of his admirers. Still, there was no
lack of skeptics, who remained unconvinced. Some of
Rilke's critics even feel justified to talk about his
"pathological nobility mania." The legend that his an-
cestors descended from the Von Rülekes of Carinthia
is based on vague rumors only.

The fantasies about their blue blood had already
been whispered into the boy's ears by his mother.
Admittedly, to belong to nobility was of some practical
value within the society in which she moved and to
which she aspired for her son. Her brother-in-law
Jaroslaw Rilke, who was a particularly zealous re-
searcher into their ancestry, was so filled with high-
flown ambitions that those considerations alone were
a good part of the reason he eagerly desired the nim-
bus of knighthood. The notary Jaroslaw von Rilke (he
was permitted to use the "von" after the "renewed"
bestowal of nobility) possessed, next to his genealogi-
cal interests, a great deal of practical concern for his
family. He also aided his nephew René. It was mainly
due to his efforts that René was given money to help
him with his studies, even after he had given up law
school.

Viewed against the social background of the Austrian hierarchy, Rilke's preoccupation with nobility
can be understood more readily. In the declining
empire of the Hapsburgs, the aristocracy still determined the "higher" style of life and one's social status,
reaching all the way down to waiters and doormen. A
small episode that the Princess Marie von Thurn und

Taxis tells in her memoirs illuminates the social scene. Wishing to provide Rilke, who was her protégé, with an artistic treat reserved for court circles only, she took him along as her companion to one of the concerts in the chapel of the Wiener Burg, the emperor's residence. It was obviously not sufficient credential to introduce her charge—who, in 1915, was already a famous writer—simply as such. For the benefit of the uniformed Cerberus who guarded the entrance to this closed society, she identified Rilke as her "nephew, the Baron von Rilke." Rilke's allegedly noble descent proved useful on other occasions, not so peripheral in nature. Practical considerations may have been far from Rilke's mind, yet the luster of his noble ancestry was a welcome addition in the shaping of his life style. In "Selbstbildnis" (Self-Portrait), part of the *Neue Gedichte* (New Poems), published in 1907, he says about himself:

> The old and noble family
> Firming his eyebrow's build
> His glance still blue
> And filled
> With childhood's fears . . .[2]

After an interlude as a pupil in a business school in Linz, René returned to the city of his birth. There, urged on by his uncle, he belatedly passed his examinations and graduated. He then enrolled at the Karls-University in Prague as a student of law. Having relinquished the dream of a military career for René, his family now hoped that he would someday take over the law practice of his successful uncle. René's

initial enthusiasm for his studies, however, did not last
long. Rather than attending his legal lectures, he followed his inner voice. This voice beckoned him to a
world beyond a bourgeois career. In the culturally
lively atmosphere of the German inhabitants of
Prague, the young man found companions in his poetic endeavors within the Concordia, a society for arts
and literature that staged poetry readings and arranged theatrical events and concerts.

During those years in Prague, which lasted until
1896, Rilke published several volumes of poetry,
stories, and even some experiments in drama. Upon
reexamination, Rilke rejected a large part of his early
efforts and admitted only a fraction into his total
work. His first publication, *Leben und Lieder: Bilder
und Tagebuchblätter* (Life and Songs: Pictures and
Notes from a Diary), had appeared in print as early
as 1894. It was followed by the volumes *Larenopfer*
(Sacrifice to the Lares), published in 1896 when he
was living in Munich, and *Traumgekrönt* (Dream-
crown), published in 1897 when he was living in Berlin. These latter two volumes of poetry were not
completely repudiated by Rilke in later years.

Local critics handed Rilke his first laurels. Critics
with more severe standards accused his early poetry
of agreeable blandness and talked of it as having
"romanticizing" and "catholicizing" tendencies, a supposition based on a misunderstanding. In this early
poetry, Rilke was less concerned with content than
with a certain perfection of form. His smooth creations, verse that flowed easily from his pen, probably

covered up some sentimental banalities. But the pleasingly sentimental sold well, then as now, and the young Rilke—and here all his interpreters agree—was said to be quite industrious and adroit in marketing his books. Rilke seems to have felt that his excessive and youthful striving for success was justified by the necessity of giving positive reports on his progress to parents and relatives. Added to this, however, there is an objective factor that explains the ephemeral character of his early poetry: his still immature personality succumbed to the intellectual climate of the turn of the century. The youth of that time, searching for new æsthetic formulas and shapes, delighted in discoveries of the unusual, in mannerisms that exalted the ornamental and decorative. Prague did not remain untouched by all this. Exhibits and literary evenings introduced the "modern" into Prague.

Maurice Maeterlinck, the Belgian compatriot of the jugendstil master Henry van de Velde, was the idol of the æstheticizing poets and one of the first to inspire Rilke. This scion of an immensely wealthy patrician family of Ghent luxuriated in mysticism. In his works he ranged from the mood of Christian legends to heathen Dionysian hymns. (Jugendstil in Germany, like the secession style in Austria and art nouveau in France and Belgium, was a movement by artists to reject naturalism in favor of idealized styling divorced from everyday life. Primarily movements in the graphic arts and architecture, they influenced writers.) The youthful literary sins charged to Rilke, can, for the most part, be traced to the influence of

neoromanticism. The same holds true for his minor
dramas and scenic sketches, such as *Im Frühfrost* (In
the Early Frost), or works such as *Dämmerung*
(Dusk) or *Ohne Gegenwart* (Without a Present).

In his poses, too, the young René Rilke showed
himself to be an apt pupil of neoromantic decadent
dandyism, as it appeared in Paris, London, or Brussels.
Rilke could be seen strolling along the Graben, the
promenade of Prague, wearing an elegant Prince
Albert coat with a stand-up collar. In his hand was a
long-stemmed flower that he carried ahead of him
like a sacrificial candle.

Even though Rilke's poems were dominated by
neoromanticism and symbolic æstheticism, he sometimes achieved purer and simpler verse by using meta-
phorical language derived from the life of the people.
Pure jugendstil, however, are stanzas like this, which
appeared in the volume of poems *Sacrifice to the
Lares*:

> Blissfully dreamy vigil.
> Now night engulfs the lands;
> The moon, a pale white lily
> Unfolds between her hands.[3]

Rilke believed in the power of night, as he later
confessed in his *Stundenbuch* (The Book of Hours).
He may have felt the Lares to be guardian spirits.
And yet he was not at all only dominated by precious
melancholia. Despite a certain snobbishness, compassion for others and social concern emerged early in
life. One of his early poems even found its way into
an anthology of contemporary proletarian verse:

Every maiden waits for love
When the trees turn green above.
We must forever sew and stitch
Until our eyes are burning. . . .[4]

Quite in contrast to the picture of the "lonely poet" that has come down to us from the later Rilke, his years in Prague were filled with social life and even with a certain amount of organizing activities. He planned to found an association of "Modern Artists of the Imagination." He offered himself—for the most part successfully—to the publishing houses and periodicals as a steady contributor, and he strove to surround himself with likeminded spirits. In a letter to a young female feuilletonist, he went so far as to announce in rhymed verse one of his high-flown projects.

Rilke even succeeded in interesting a Berlin ensemble in producing his one-act play, *In the Early Frost*, which staged the work in the Deutsche Volkstheater in Prague. In it appeared a German actor, still unknown at that time—Max Reinhardt. But the play found no favor with the public.

In his *Zwei Prager Geschichten* (1899; Two Prague Stories) Rilke revealed himself as an expert on the unique atmosphere of Prague. He loved its crooked alleys, its "golden" domes, its historic silhouette. In the light of this, it seems even stranger that he had so little use for the city of his birth in later years and visited it rarely. Neither did he, later in life, give much thought to his Prague teachers: the critic Alfred Klaar; the poets Friedrich Adler and

Hugo Salus; the German professor August Sauer of
the Prague University, who predicted a great future
for him. In a letter to the historian Hermann Pongs,
written in 1924, Rilke once discussed the years of his
youth, talking about them as "hasty years." He admitted that he "had disclaimed his early stage with a
certain embarrassment."

As the "strongest hand he was privileged to grasp"
he named a North German, the poet Detlev von
Liliencron, who delighted his young admirer several
times in his letters by addressing him as "my magnifi-
cent René Maria." Rilke showed his gratitude to
Liliencron, who was in constant financial difficulties,
by organizing lectures for him, and defending him
wherever he could. Thanks to Liliencron, Rilke expe-
rienced his first contact with the more reserved temperament of the German and Scandinavian north.

This receptivity to a point of view reaching into
mysticism is, from then on, discernible in Rilke's work,
especially in works of his middle period. Prague, however, with its special aura that reinforced the visions
of other poets, is to be found in only a few of Rilke's
early impressions. Too many painful memories
marred the past. His childhood was, for him, linked
with a dark feeling of fear that remained with him
for life. There was nothing that could make the young
Rilke remain in Prague permanently. Family life was
irksome to him; the provincialism could not satisfy
him. In addition to all this, his mother had separated
from his father and had gone to Vienna to live nearer
the court, nearer to the world of her dreams. (Rumor

has it that Phia Rilke was always dressed entirely in black, in an attire similar to that worn by widowed duchesses.) Because his mother was there, Vienna held no attraction for the young Rilke, and his first move was to Munich.

2

Munich ...

Berlin ...

Russia ...

In 1896 and 1897 Rilke studied for two semesters in Munich. For him "study" meant to follow up in various ways the stimulations of diverse disciplines. He was, however, most interested in the history of art. Only rarely did he take part in the doings of the bohemian life in Schwabing, a district of Munich that was then the student quarter. His friendships were usually fleeting, as were those with the poet Wilhelm von Scholz, son of the Prussian minister, and with Jakob Wassermann, who had already attained success.

It was through Wassermann that Rilke became aware of several writers who were to prove important for his poetic development. Reading Turgenev first opened his eyes to Russia. He was moved even more by the prose writings of the Danish poet Jens Peter Jacobsen, with whom he felt such close affinity that he found it difficult to accept the fact that Jacobsen had died of consumption in 1885. Like him, Rilke shared an oversensitivity to the demands of everyday life, an obsession with the idea of death, a "great sadness," an honesty to the point of self-destruction, and a yearning for quiet. Rilke's poems in the volume *Dream-crown* (1897) as well as some novellas and sketches in *Am Leben hin* (1898; By the Side of Life), reveal the influence of Jacobsen.

Of all Rilke's human encounters in Munich, the one with Lou Andreas-Salomé proved to be the most enduring. Lou Andreas-Salomé was a towering figure, far ahead of her day. She was born in Saint Petersburg in 1861, daughter of a Russian general, Salomé, who was of Huguenot extraction. She was married to the Oriental scholar Friedrich Andreas, who taught first at the University of Berlin and then, from 1903 on, in Göttingen. (Lou Andreas-Salomé died there in 1937, a few years after her husband.) While still young, she became known as the writer of controversial books about Nietzsche (whom she had befriended) and Ibsen. By the time she met Rilke in Munich she had already published short stories, most of which were psychological studies of complex women. Sigmund Freud, to whom she later dedicated her book *Dank an Freud,* called his spirited advocate, whose influence extended beyond the circle of professional experts, a "perceiver par excellence."

Rilke's lifelong friendship with Lou led him onto new paths. He found in her not only the direct resonance of an understanding human being, but a means of participation in the world, one who pulled him out of the solitary life style he was being drawn to. He regarded her, who lived what in those days was considered a completely emancipated life, less as a mistress than as a long-desired mother figure who provided him with solace and refuge. "My strength, my all" he called his friend. This fascinating woman, who was devoted to more than purely intellectual adventures, was also the first to encourage his farflung travels. When she left Munich, where she had owned a summer home in the Isar Valley, Rilke suffered from such loneliness that he followed her to Berlin and shortly thereafter to Russia.

During the years he spent in Munich Rilke be-

came more particular about his dealings with the contemporary literary public than he had been in Prague.
He was forced to live in rather restricted circumstances, and led the sad existence of a boarder. Although he now made more exacting demands on his
own work, he did not altogether refrain from trying to
reach a public. He published a periodical called
Wegwarten, of which, however, only three issues appeared. Richard Dehmel, the magnanimous protector
of every young talent, who was asked to contribute,
wrote that *Wegwarten* was designed to offer pure
lyric poetry. Rilke also contributed to other literary
periodicals.

Rilke's connections with the Schwabing salons
were mostly short-lived, as for instance with the salon
of the Countess Franziska Reventlow, a writer who
had taken up bohemian life after her divorce, or with
that of Frieda von Bülow, who advocated free love in
her poems.

After his stay in Munich in 1897, Rilke no longer
signed his name as René, but as "Rainer Maria Rilke."
He had become enamored with the rhythm and sound
of this name. The new name marked a new beginning
for him: one of an ever more consciously pursued personal style of life.

Rilke was still a student, and he remained a student in Berlin. There he attended, erratically, lectures
in philosophy and history given by Georg Simmel, an
artistically inclined sociologist and subtly differentiat-
ing analyst of concepts, and by the philosopher Kurt
Breysig, who has been called the German Toynbee
because of his theories of historical development. One

should not underestimate the influence those two scholars had on Rilke, especially since Breysig's demands for "artistry in the historian" met with Rilke's ideas of the connections between the history of art and history in general.

In Berlin, Rilke at first took a room in Wilmersdorf. But very soon he felt drawn to move nearer to Lou Andreas-Salomé, who was living close to the Roseneck in Schmargendorf, in a villa called Waldfrieden. At the turn of the century, this region was a rural idyll. Country lanes led into the Grunewald forest, where deer came close to the roadside to be fed by the strollers. Rilke often accompanied Lou and her husband on those walks, or he and Lou went alone.

In the fall of 1899, on a stormy November night in Berlin, Rilke wrote *The Lay of the Love and Death of Cornet Christopher Rilke*, probably his most famous work. The small volume, however, did not appear in print until 1906. This prose poem, which was a favorite for recitation and which was popularized by the Youth Movement, was based on exacting historical studies, as the Berlin publisher Wolfgang Paul discovered recently. A number of other prose works and several poems were also written in Berlin: a major part of the poetry volume *Mir zur Feier* (Celebration of Myself); the first part of *The Book of Hours*; and, in the early part of 1900, his last attempt at drama, *Das tägliche Leben* (Daily Life), which was tinged with social criticism. This drama remained as unsuccessful as his others.

Lou Andreas-Salomé introduced Rilke into the

intellectual and artistic world of Berlin. There he
associated with writers Gerhart Hauptmann, Richard
Dehmel, and Stefan George, without, however, enter-
ing into a close relationship with any one of them.
When he chose a friend, it was the relatively unknown
Carl Hauptmann (brother of Gerhart), a mystic and
the author of the novel *Einhart der Lächler*. Stefan
George remained deliberately reserved toward Rilke,
which was not true of the mighty Gerhart Hauptmann.
Only much later, in Florence, did Rilke and George,
who did not respond to Rilke's charm, settle down to
a serious talk.

For the most part, Rilke avoided the Berlin
salons, as he was later to avoid Parisian salons. A
certain shyness, which had begun to develop during
the years in Munich, now deepened. Still, a spirit
like Rilke's—by no means unaffected by the trends of
his time—could hardly stay outside the strong cur-
rents of the German capital. Berlin was not only the
main traffic center for the German art and literature
of the day, but also a testing ground for young talent.
Here the various literary factions took doctrinal posi-
tions and the most diverse tendencies overlapped—
naturalism to neoromanticism; realism and naturalism
to the esoteric spracherneuerung (a movement devoted to language revival). Into this chorus of voices
entered Rilke's "new, enticingly lyrical sound," as
Thomas Mann described it. Rilke, for his part, recognized the importance of Thomas Mann early, and in a
review of *Buddenbrooks* paid homage to it as an ep-
ochal work. In fact *The Notebooks of Malte Laurids
Brigge*, which appeared ten years after *Buddenbrooks*,

has certain features similar to Mann's early novel, with its decadent mood. Rilke gladly accepted the manifold stimulations Berlin had to offer, but Berlin, no more than Munich, could hold him for any length of time. Here too, inner restlessness drove him away. As Munich had been the starting point for his first visits to Italy, so Berlin now became the base for his visits to Russia, made in the company of Lou.

Rilke's first Russian journey lasted from April to June 1899. Even before embarking on this trip, he voiced an almost enraptured enthusiasm for Russia. He wanted to spend Easter in Moscow so that "the sound from the Kremlin churches may crown my devout observance." His second and last trip lasted from May to August 1900. He viewed Russia not as a tourist, but as a pilgrim. In one of his enthusiastic letters he wrote:

I have heard the church bells in Moscow at Easter time and I sense the breath of spring in the shimmering birch groves and the rushing waters of the vast Neva. I find every day to be a strange, moving experience among these people who are so full of reverence and piety, and I rejoice in this new experience.

To the painter Leonid Pasternak, Boris Pasternak's father, Rilke wrote that he looked forward to Russia "as a child looks forward to Christmas." His enthusiasm for the Russian people and for Russian literature also expressed itself in practical ways, for instance in his efforts to establish communications between Austrian and Russian artists and between Russian writers and the Viennese periodical *Ver sacrum*.

Through diligent studies, Rilke mastered enough of the Russian language to be able to read Russian books, and, within limits, to carry on a conversation. After his return from Russia he also translated from the Russian and even made an attempt to write poems in that language. He was well acquainted with the Russian poets Pushkin and Lermontov and felt a personal attachment to Anton Chekhov.

A high point in Rilke's pilgrimage was a visit to Lev Tolstoi. He described in a rather reserved way this meeting in Yasnaya Polyana in a letter to Sophia Schill, dated May 1900. Sophia Schill, a Russian friend of the Andreases, had been instrumental in getting Tolstoi to receive Rilke. Rilke wrote:

A servant took our calling cards inside. After a while we saw the count's figure in the dim anteroom. The oldest son opened the glass door, and we were in the hall facing the count, this aged man, whom one would always approach as a son, even if one did not want to stay under his fatherly powers.

The last sentence already denotes the tone of rebellion against parental authority and the burden of being loved that emerges at the end of *The Notebooks of Malte Laurids Brigge*. Language difficulties seemed to have emerged during the visit. Tolstoi talked almost exclusively with Lou Andreas-Salomé and hardly addressed his young admirer.

In *Safe Conduct*, the title given his memoirs, Boris Pasternak, who was then still a child, recalls having met Lou Andreas-Salomé and Rilke:

Shortly before our departure, a man dressed in a black Tyrolean cape stepped up to the window of our compartment; with him was a tall woman. The woman exchanged an occasional word of Russian with my mother, but the stranger spoke only German. Although I knew this language well, I had never heard it spoken in quite this way. That is why this man—in the midst of the crowds that thronged the platforms between the first and the second departure signals—appeared to me like a silhouette among bodies, like fiction in the thicket of reality. . . .

The Book of Hours and the *Geschichten vom lieben Gott* (Stories of God; first published as *Vom lieben Gott und Anderes* [About God and Other Things]), written under the impression of his Russian pilgrimage, are, to some degree, imbued with the true spirit of the simple Russian people, who were on the whole naively religious. Rilke, however, tended to idealize the Russian "humaneness." For the most part, he saw Russia through the medium of its literature, though he may have spoken to many unsophisticated people in his pilgrimage, which took him as far as the Volga. For a few days he even lived in the primitive hut of a peasant-poet who was a disciple of Tolstoi.

It is difficult to decide to which of the two giants of Russian literature Rilke felt more indebted: to the prophet of a new Christianity, Tolstoi the rigorous moralist, or to the suffering, soul-searching Dostoyevski. It almost seems as if the mystical, God-seeking quality of Dostoyevski did, after all, mean more to Rilke. One thing is certain—the creator of *The Book of Hours* and the Tolstoian-sounding *Stories of God* revered the spirit of Old Russia with almost childlike love. It is in terms of this emotion that Rilke's confession—"The Old Russia has forever been cemented into the foundations of my life"—can be understood.

As a mature man, at the height of his fame, Rilke still kept speaking of his "adopted home, Russia." This greatly surprised his friends, for he scarcely ever mentioned his native Bohemia, which after all was Slavic, too. The "Buch vom mönchischen Leben" (Of Monastic Life), the first part of *The Book of Hours*, was written in 1899 under the influence of his first Russian journey. It was followed in 1901 by the second part, "Buch von der Pilgerschaft" (Of Pilgrimage), and in 1903 by the third part, "Das Buch von der Armut und dem Tode" (Of Poverty and Death). Rilke comes close to mystic identification when he says: "The cloth my life is made of is the same as all the dying hours of the czars of old."

Besides his translations of modern Russian poets, there are other poetic documents of Rilke's pilgrimage. Among them is his version of the old epic poem *Lay of Prince Igor*, which was also set to music.

Rilke ascribed an historic mission to the Russian people. In a letter to his traveling companion, Lou Andreas-Salomé, he wrote: "Maybe the Russian has been created to let human history pass him by, so that he may, later on, fall in with the harmony of things. . . ."

The mysticism of Rilke's early years, far removed from traditional religious beliefs, had its origins in the perhaps ambiguous and often misunderstood Russian Orthodox faith, which Rilke may have understood. In Rilke's language, however, the "religious" confession in *The Book of Hours* seems new and bold: "I revolve around God, the ancient tower, and I circle for thousands of years."

3

North-German Interlude: Worpswede

In lyrical and allegorical language, Rilke described the place and the landscape of his stay in North Germany. In Worpswede, which had been an artists' colony since 1889, he hoped to find inner composure and self-assurance. He envisioned "a life of profundity and simplicity."

In 1900 the painter and illustrator of books, Heinrich Vogeler, invited Rilke (who was an admirer of secession paintings) into his home. In the circle of Worpswede artists Rilke met the sculptor Clara Westhoff (a pupil of Rodin) and her friend the painter Paula Becker. (Paula, under the name of Paula Modersohn-Becker, was the only one of the Worpswede artists to achieve permanent fame.)

At no other time in his life, not even in the later Paris years, was Rilke as close to sculptors and painters as he was in Worpswede. The two women, the tall, dark sculptor and the blonde painter, whom the Worpswede friends regarded almost as sisters, played an intriguing role in Rilke's life. Rilke showed the same affection for both. Both women charmed him equally, and he could not at first decide between them. If we follow the pages of his diary, it almost appears as if he had been drawn more strongly to Paula. Rilke relates long talks with her. He even indulges in such turns of speech as "the beauty of all experience, of braving death and of desiring death, of eternity and why we feel a kinship with the eternal." In pure jugendstil he praises Paula's hair "of Florentine gold" and her voice, which "had folds of silk."

Rilke's affection may, in the beginning, have

tended to favor Paula Becker, but Paula was already engaged to the Worpswede landscape painter Otto Modersohn and did not indicate any willingness to dissolve this bond. In the face of Paula's seemingly wavering affection, Rilke hesitated to declare himself to Clara Westhoff. Clara's boyishness attracted him, yet probably evoked mixed feelings. At any rate, one fine day, torn by conflicting sentiments, he hastily departed for Berlin, where Paula Becker had also gone for a short stay. As a consequence of his move to Worpswede and his new relationships, the bonds of his friendship to Lou Andreas-Salomé had loosened. Therefore he was especially close to Paula during this Berlin visit. Paula's diaries, however, make it perfectly clear that her relationship to Rilke hardly ever overstepped the boundaries of comradely sympathy. Although she listened when he read his poetry to her, she was emotionally apart from him. Her friendly interest in Rilke's work did not carry her far enough to find the key to the strangely heightened lyricism of his poetry, and that understanding was something he desired with all his heart. Her less complex nature found Rilke's artistic language too complicated, and his entire personality basically mystifying.

Paula Modersohn-Becker was probably the only woman who ever felt close to Rilke without paying homage to him. In her diary she expressed herself quite bluntly:

Rainer Maria Rilke, a fine lyrical talent, delicate and sensitive, with small, pathetic hands. He read from his poems, tender and full of premonitions. Sweet and pale. The two men [Otto Mondersohn and Rilke] could, in the final analysis, not understand one another. The battle between realism and idealism. . . .

She also voiced criticism about the organlike sound of the *Stories of God.*

Paula's entry about her friend Clara Westhoff's marriage to Rilke sounds short and resigned: "C. W. now has a husband. I no longer seem to belong to her life."

With almost harsh frankness Paula wrote to Rilke after his marriage, in a note thanking him for the present of a book: "I thank you very much, dear friend, for your beautiful book. And please, I beg you, do not present us with riddles. We, my husband and I, are two simple people. Solving puzzles is difficult for us and afterward our heads ache and our hearts."

On April 24, 1901, Rainer Maria Rilke married Clara Westhoff. A daughter, Ruth, was born to them. The marriage of these two unusual people was not a union in the conventional sense. Their life together was of short duration, though Rilke never allowed their marriage to be terminated by divorce.

A letter to Paula Modersohn-Becker reveals Rilke's attitude toward his own marriage and marriage in general:

I too stand quietly and full of deep confidence before the gates of this solitude, because this I consider the highest aim of a union between two people: that each guards the solitude of the other. If it is characteristic of indifference and the crowds not to acknowledge solitude, it is the task of love and friendship to constantly provide the opportunities for it. And only those are the true unions, which rhythmically interrupt deep solitudes.

Those lines correspond to the basic beliefs of *The Notebooks of Malte Laurids Brigge.*

How skeptically Rilke viewed married bliss can be seen from another letter:

Anyhow, I am of the opinion that marriage as such does not deserve as much emphasis as has been given it in the course of its conventional development. It would occur to no one to demand of a single person that he be happy, but if a person marries, one is surprised if he is *not* happy.

Maybe Rilke had hoped to find a true home in Worpswede. In a letter to Clara Westhoff shortly before their marriage he wrote: "From the very beginning, your homeland was more to me than a benevolent stranger. It simply was home, with people living there. (Most people live in alien lands and all the homelands are empty.)"

In neighboring Westerwede, Rilke and Clara moved into a thatched peasant hut. But the newly founded household proved to be a haven only so long as a check from Prague arrived every month. As soon as the Rilkes realized that the restless René had permanently discontinued his studies, they withdrew their assistance. Rilke was now forced to fend for himself and to take care of a wife and child. He was tireless in letting all the world know of his plight and asking for assistance to obtain steady employment. He offered his services as lecturer and translator; he wrote a festival scene for the opening of the Bremen Art Exhibition Hall. For the Bremen Art Gallery he even acted as stage director of Maeterlinck's play *Sister Beatrix.* He owed this assignment mainly to the patronage of Gustav Pauli, the director of the Bremen

Art Gallery. It was also through Pauli that he was commissioned to write a monograph about Worpswede for the publishing house of Velhagen and Clasing. But these earnings did not help much.

The introduction to Rilke's monograph on Worpswede pays homage to the school of romantic landscape painting, most of all to the painter Philipp Otto Runge. Rilke saw the Worpswede painters as close to Millet and Segantini, who were preimpressionist artists. Rilke describes the landscape of Worpswede as if he were seeing it through the eyes of a painter.

But he also saw the people, the peat cutters. In the face of their harsh fate, Rilke asked: What are painters doing among these people? With sober realism Rilke noted the social contrast between the artists and their models. "They [the artists] come from far away, they put these people—who are not like themselves—into the landscape; not much force is needed. The strength of a child is enough . . . they reach for the best and have turned into children."

4

*Paris
and Rodin*

When Rainer Maria Rilke left Worpswede and Westerwede, he also left behind him the only life among family and friends that was ever to be granted him. Yet it was not a "new existence" that lay before him. As uncertain as the future may have looked, he was nevertheless determined to continue to fashion his life into a work of art, to style his own biography, and to forgo a bourgeois career.

After an extended stay with one of his earliest aristocratic patrons, the Prince Schönaich-Carolath, at the Castle Haseldorf in Holstein, Rilke went to Paris in August 1902. The first thing he wanted to do was to visit Auguste Rodin so that he could utilize their conversations for a monograph on Rodin he was planning to write. In the letter introducing himself to Rodin, he had made a point of the fact that his young wife, Clara Westhoff, had briefly been Rodin's pupil: "Not far from you and the eternity that is the aura of your person."

Rilke rented a room in a narrow alley in the Latin Quarter and feverishly awaited the day that "may turn out to be the happiest day" of his life, meaning the day of his first visit to Rodin's studio. While he waited for the day to arrive, he looked around Paris. As he wrote to Clara, the big city was very, very alien to him. "The many hospitals around here strike me with fear. I can understand why they appear constantly in Verlaine, Baudelaire, and Mallarmé." In *The Notebooks of Malte Laurids Brigge* he describes this mood: "So this is where people come to live. To me, it seems more as if one died here."

After his loneliness, the visit to Rodin's Paris studio was a ray of light. "He was benevolent and mild-mannered and I felt as if I had always known him." The day after his first visit to Rodin's home in Meudon, however, he wrote: "The villa is not beautiful at all." Not far from the house, in a tremendous hall, Rilke saw Rodin's studio, which made "a great and strange impression" on him. The studio was overflowing with sculptures, which Rilke admired dutifully. At mealtime it struck him as strange that he was neither introduced to the lady of the house nor to the other guests. About Rodin's wife he wrote: "Madame Rodin, looking tired, irritated, nervous and listless. . . ." A quarrel between Rodin and his wife, at the table in front of their guests, saddened him. Afterward, the hours of viewing sculptures wearied him further. "Because everything is white, one walks among these many blinding plasters in the extremely light pavilion as if in snow. My eyes hurt. . . ."

About Rodin himself, Rilke wrote: "Rodin talked about art, about the merchants of art, about his lonely position." When they were looking at the garden, Rodin's small daughter placed a snail in her father's hand. This Rodin used to develop his thoughts on art: "Here, objects do not deceive. This little snail reminds me of the great works of Greek art; it has the same simplicity, the same smoothness, the same inner glow, the same joyous and festive kind of surface. . . ."

Rodin even indulged in some personal confidence in his first long talk with Rilke. To be an artist is to be lonely, he said. Friends only disappoint, and he had

married "because one must have a wife." At the end
of the conversation, he gave Rilke the advice: "One
must work, nothing but work."

The fascination Rodin exerted on Rilke is more
comprehensible when one takes into account Rilke's
propensity for identifying with his ideal of the
moment. Even the first sentences of his glorifying
essays about Rodin make this clear. "Rodin was lonely
before he was famous, and the fame that he achieved
may have made him even more lonely. For fame is,
after all, only the essence of all the misunderstandings
that collect around a new name." The last sentence
especially holds a clue to an interpretation of Rilke.
It was Rilke who felt misunderstood. Rodin, however,
did not feel misunderstood on at least one point: his
appeal to an affluent public. He was the highest paid
sculptor of his time. Kings and millionaires gave him
their commissions. Through Rilke's mediation, he ne-
gotiated to sculpt Gerhart Hauptmann. The price of
the portrait bust was to be ten thousand gold francs.
The fact that this commission failed to materialize
was not because of the high price, but because of
Hauptmann's doubts. He did not want to risk being
sculpted in a way he might not approve of.

Undoubtedly, Rilke thought too highly of Rodin's
work. Rodin was not the Michelangelo of the bourgeois era, which he seems to have felt himself to be.
His monumental structures were still influenced by
the eclectic historicism of the nineteenth century. To
be sure, a great span of development separates Rodin's
beginnings, including his often pathetic nudes, from

the expressive "Burghers of Calais" and his powerful Balzac. Fundamentally he was a romantic philistine who, as in his presumptuous essay on the Gothic cathedrals of France, tried to rise above himself in his art. As far as his humanity was concerned he failed, as Rilke's painful experience was to show.

The confusing and depressing city atmosphere of Paris was the background for Rilke's "activities," which consisted of concentrated watching and learning. He came to recognize the dual face of this so-called "Mecca of civilization." True, Paris, especially in those years of an oncoming revolution in the arts, was a center of world culture. But at the same time it was one of the most socially backward agglomerations of human habitations in the whole world, a blighted giant of a city, to whose decaying charms Rilke's artistic sensibilities succumbed hopelessly. Rainer Maria Rilke knew and sensed more than the vibrations and halftones of the impressionists, who let nature triumph above all. He saw behind the macabre merriment of the Parisians. Toulouse-Lautrec could be charmed by the melancholy wisdom of the children of the streets, but it only saddened Rilke. Following Rodin's advice, he practiced discipline in his work and an unsentimental view of nature. Primarily, thanks to Rodin's example, he shaped his language into a more rigorous instrument of expression. And this in spite of the often contradictory and sometimes debilitating atmosphere of Paris. Rilke learned, in Robert Musil's words, "how porcelain turns into marble."

In the first version of Rilke's *Das Buch der Bilder*
(The Book of Pictures), published in 1902, one finds
some poems that are perfect in the brevity of their
statement and the restrained melody of their language. One of these is the poem "Herbsttag" (Autumn
Day), which rightly is considered one of the most
beautiful poems in the German language and is
quoted repeatedly. "Lord: it is time. The summer was
so vast. . ."

Another is "Ernste Stunde" (Grave Hour). Here
speaks Rilke, who, in a *unio mystica*, feels himself
painfully akin with all humanity. It is characteristic of
Rilke's mode of work that the theme of this poem,
which is made up of only four stanzas, occupied his
mind for years. The first two stanzas were written in
1899, the last two in about 1902.

> Who now weeps anywhere in the world,
> Without cause weeps in the world,
> Weeps about me.[5]

Paris signified the decisive break in Rilke's life.
Except for his extensive journeys, the city on the Seine
remained his home until the outbreak of World War I.
The first part of his *The Book of Pictures* still contains much impressionism and sublimated mood. Some
of the poems in this volume had been written prior
to his time in Paris. This shows in the titles, which
still have the sound of youth: "Die Engel" (The Angels), "Mädchenmelancholie" (Maidenly Melancholy),
"Bangnis" (Anxiety), "Klage" (Lament), "Einsam-
keit" (Loneliness), "Am Rande der Nacht" (At the
Edge of Night).

But Rilke's new style was already discernible in "Fragmente aus verlorenen Tagen" (Fragments from Lost Days), written in Paris. This is an almost lyrical introduction to *The Notebooks of Malte Laurids Brigge*, the work in which he strove to express all there was to say. Motivated by his Paris experiences are also the songs of the beggar, the blind man, the drunkard, the suicide, the widow, the idiot, the orphan, the dwarf, and the leper. But towering above them all remains the confession of the poem "Grave Hour."

> Who now dies anywhere in the world,
> Without cause dies in the world,
> Looks at me.[6]

It was not until his move to Paris that Rilke considered his letters as part of his work. Letters also replaced his diaries, and more and more, they turned into an accompaniment to his poems. Often the themes of his verse or prose appear first in his letters. In the form of correspondence he renewed the bond with Lou Andreas-Salomé, and through his letters Clara was made a witness to the solitude he had chosen for himself. Although his letters are mainly concerned with his poetic productions, they are revealing documents of the era, thanks to Rilke's frankness and his gift for perspicacious insights. Whatever he criticizes becomes graphic. He writes "Paris is vain, ornamented with mirrors."

The paintings of the Louvre and the literature in the National Library, where he read Baudelaire, Flaubert, and the Goncourts, were the great and beautiful that compensated for all that was dark and depressing. And so he decides: "I will stay in Paris for the time being, just because it is difficult. . . ." In the final days of 1902 he finished an essay on Rodin; he was to write a second one several years later. But he still did not feel at home in Paris: "Thus must have been the cities God's wrath created. . ." he wrote to Otto Modersohn. "To all this, Rodin represents a great, quiet, powerful contrast."

Rilke made several journeys out of Paris, in 1903 and 1904. His accounts, especially in letters written in the spring of 1903, are often coolly sober. In Italy he, the oversensitive, was annoyed at the German tourists who were even then flooding the country. The showy splendor of the spas along the Ligurian coast seemed artificial and overdone to him. He detested the "southern temperament." In Viareggio he finally found lodgings off the beaten track, and had the use of a straw hut on the beach, from which he could watch the play of the waves. Here he could also swim without feeling importuned. His choice of reading matter already pointed north: "Only Jacobsen is always in my pocket; he reads beautifully down here."

As an early adherent of nudism, Rilke loved to sunbathe naked in the evening, but was afraid of attracting unpleasant attention. He said that "in an emergency" he would put on the top of his bathing suit. "The emergency is the English woman who may show up anywhere."

5

The

Wanderer

of the

Stundenbuch

In April 1903 Rilke wrote the third and final part of *The Book of Hours*, called "Of Poverty and Death." His changed circumstances, his moving from one place to another, are reflected in this part of the book, which is less emotional and more reflective than the parts preceding it, "Of Monastic Life" and "Of Pilgrimage." The third book mirrors the sadness of the early days in Paris. More a beseeching gesture than a prayer, actually a cry to God, to a distant, unknown God, are these lines of verse:

> For, Lord, the giant cities are
> Lost ones and disassembled;
> The greatest flee before the flames,
> There is no comfort, no respite,
> Their scant time has but ended.[7]

In this poem Rilke's compassion appears with great intensity. The desperate plea rings out:

> O Lord, grant each his own death.
> The dying that befits each life
> That gave him love, intent, and sorrow.[8]

In the third book, we find a line that is often misinterpreted: "For poverty is a great glow within."[9] When critics of Rilke take this sentence out of context, they feel justified in seeing the poet as an esoteric thinker, without social ties. The satirist George Grosz, who used this line as a caption under one of his drawings of misery, probably never read the third book, much less the complete *The Book of Hours*. The critics do not take into account the fact that this line is followed by a long poem in which he describes his

46

own inner feelings more clearly and with greater depth. (The "you" is his self-address.)

> You are the beggar, you the poor one,
> You are the stone that has no place,
> You are the outcast and the leper,
> Who moves his rattle through the city.[10]

These lines show that the "glow within" bears solely on Rilke's own existential experience. Whether "Of Poverty and Death," which Rilke wrote during his solitude on the Italian coast, has a social message or not may be debatable. One thing though is certain: that Rilke rejected urbanized civilization, unbridled lust for money, loss of calm and moderation, and the broken lives of the city dwellers crushed by the conditions of their time. Rilke comes close to dreamlike, chiliastic visions of a peaceful, final state when he says of the poor:

> They will endure beyond the final ending,
> Outlive the nations that have lost their goals,
> And will arise like hands well rested
> When the hands of all classes and all peoples are
>   weary.[11]

Rilke spent the summer months of 1903 with his wife in the old Worpswede circle. In the fall of that year, he went to Rome as the guest of friends who belonged to the group of artists who had gathered around Jakob von Uexküll. While still in Rome, that is, before his trip to Jacobsen's homeland, he had started work on *The Notebooks of Malte Laurids Brigge*, a novel with a partly Nordic, partly Parisian atmosphere. Furthermore he took Rodin's advice to study classical art in Rome. At the urging of Rodin, Clara Rilke also went to Rome to continue her sculpture studies. The couple spent a brief time in Assisi, which gave them the opportunity to visit the places where the "Holy Francis let shine his radiant poverty." To him Rilke dedicated the last part of *The Book of Hours.*

Rilke's letters from Italy, telling in diary fashion of his difficulties and his grand expectations, are mostly written to Lou Andreas-Salomé.

There is more reality in a single poem that I have done to my satisfaction than there is in any of my relationships or attachments. In my creation I am true to myself, and I would like to find the strength to base my whole life on this truth.

Rilke was less disappointed with Rome than with Paris. But the accumulation of art depressed him and he remarked that Rome, for the most part, seemed to be a second-rate museum. In spite of these critical reservations, his contemplation of the antique works of art bore precious fruit in his work. In the early part of 1904 he wrote the prose poem "Orpheus, Eurydike, Hermes," which, in its final version, appeared in the periodical *Neue Rundschau.* Even if Rilke's first extended stay in Italy left few traces in his poetry, those traces were important, as shown by "Orpheus, Eurydike, Hermes," which already contains the seed of the leitmotiv for the *Sonette an Orpheus* (Sonnets to Orpheus) written in 1922.

Until the end of June 1904 Rilke lived in a studio outside the gates of Rome—first with his wife, then alone. While he was still in Rome he learned Danish, in order to be able to read Kierkegaard and his beloved Jens Peter Jacobsen in the original. In contrast to the harsh intellectual climate of Scandinavia, the sultry, languid atmosphere of the south enervated him. The literary Italy of that time, which stood under the star of D'Annunzio, had nothing to offer Rilke. He spoke disparagingly of the *"Gartenlaube* prettiness" (*Gartenlaube* was a wholesome family magazine of the time) of D'Annunzio's poetry.

Although *Stories of God*, published in 1904, found a friendly, sometimes even enthusiastic reception, Rilke still felt unsure of himself and was grateful for every sign of recognition. He was especially pleased with the response to his book in Sweden, where Ellen Key, the suffragette and sociology teacher, championed it. She wrote to him that his Swedish audience, though small, wanted to meet him. She arranged a lecture tour in Sweden and an invitation for Rilke to stay at a country estate.

In a letter to Ellen Key, in which he told her he would soon be going to Sweden, he wrote: "I think we . . . will soon again need the north, space, wind." He complained about the "quick, overflowing, hasty spring, that is a constant wilting and burning."

In June 1904 Rilke left Rome and went to Sweden, stopping at several places on his way. In Sweden Ellen Key had prepared that he be welcomed. In a soberly qualifying remark Rilke said dryly: "I realize that I have to accept whatever supports my existence and prolongs my chances of staying with my work.

So, being ballyhooed and heralded is surely to the good."

After stops in Worpswede and Göttingen, where he visited with Lou and her husband, he arrived in Sweden in late June. There he found the "nature of sea, plain, and sky" that Ellen Key had promised. Thanks to her recommendations, he was received like an old friend. He could pursue his work undisturbed. At first he stayed on an estate in the southern province of Schonen, later with a well-to-do family near Göteborg. In both places he was offered a great deal of consideration, help, hospitality, and unusual under-standing. He was left completely undisturbed, and his friends, who had arranged for him to give lectures— for which he undoubtedly would have been well paid —good-naturedly resigned themselves to the fact that he avoided most of these commitments. He did, how-ever, read at the Samskola, an adult college, in Göteborg in November 1904, without asking for a fee. His selection indicated what he considered suitable for a larger audience: the story of Michelangelo from *Stories of God*; the prose poem he had written in Rome, "Orpheus, Eurydike, Hermes"; three poems from *Celebration of Myself*; some things from *The Book of Pictures*, including the famous "Panther"; the poem "Herbst," written in Paris, and some stanzas he had just written in Sweden, "Abend in Skåne" (Eve-ning in Skåne).

About the mood of his audience Rilke said; "beautiful, simple, warm: full of good will and joy." After the feeling of utter loneliness that he had suf-

fered in Paris, Swedish hospitality revived in him a
friendlier outlook toward life. He expressed his thanks
in verse, in memory of the large garden of the estate
in Schonen:

> The park is high, and as if from a house
> I step out of its dimness
> Into the plain and evening. Into the wind,
> The very wind that's felt by every cloud. . . .[12]

On his way back from Sweden, Rilke visited
Copenhagen to retrace the footsteps of Jens Peter
Jacobsen.

About Copenhagen he wrote:

A unique city, strangely indescribable, dissolving into various shadings, old and yet new, frivolous and mysterious.
Everywhere, yet nowhere to be grasped, one can feel J. P.
Jacobsen, Kierkegaard, and one hears the language as if
it were interpreting all this.

Not far from Rilke's hotel in Copenhagen lived
Georg Brandes, then already the doyen of European
literary criticism and one of Nietzsche's earliest cham-
pions. To the young poet, Brandes was an almost
mythical figure. In his youth, Brandes had been a
friend of Hans Christian Andersen, the writer of fairy
tales, and he had known Flaubert and the Goncourts
in Paris. The 1905 edition of the periodical *Neue
Rundschau* contained both Georg Brandes's "Pariser
Erinnerungen" and Rilke's "Gedichte in Prosa"
(Poems in Prose) .

During his stay in Paris in 1869 and 1870, Brandes
had found that to the French, even to those well
versed in literature, German poetry was virtually un-

known, with the exception of a few poems by Goethe and Heine. It is in no small measure through Rilke that the newer German literature became more widely known in France.

Aside from the literary stimuli, Rilke's stay in Scandinavia offered him the opportunity to learn more about the progressive and eager-to-reform northern countries. He even published his views on these issues. His essay dealing with the Swedish system of education, which he recommended as exemplary and forward-looking, appeared in the Berlin periodical *Zukunft*, edited by the journalist Maximilian Harden. This article was received in a way that was greatly surprising to Rilke. In one of his letters he mentions with pride a reader's comment to the editor of *Zukunft*, in which his treatise about the Swedish school system was praised and called the best that had been written or said in Germany about school reform.

Rilke's sensitive imagination absorbed more of Scandinavia's mood than of its literature. Still, he was influenced by the Nordic literature of decadence. A title such as *Tired Souls* by the Norwegian Arne Garborg was enough to fascinate him. But he continued to value most highly Jens Peter Jacobsen's prose, suspended between dream and reality. Rilke too loved the delicate tones of musical mood-language, melting into shades of light gray.

Besides Jacobsen and Garborg, there was the Norwegian storyteller Sigbjorn Obstfelder, who had died young. Obstfelder had, in some respects, anticipated the associative prose art Rilke later used in his

The Notebooks of Malte Laurids Brigge. Rilke had read Obstfelder's *Diary of a Priest* and the volume of stories *Pilgrimage* and had discovered a kinship with its morbid characters.

When Rilke left Scandinavia in January 1905, his immediate future offered no security whatever. The only certainty he saw was "a life drenched in melancholy." Thus, one should not reproach him for accepting offers that brought his life style closer to that of his patrons. Besides, he constantly felt his health to be threatened, although he tried to live a "simple" and "natural" life. But drinking milk and walking around barefoot (he did both) were not enough to keep up his strength. An illness, not clearly diagnosed, slowly sapped his strength and finally decided his next move. He went to the Sanatorium Weißer Hirsch near Dresden for treatment. There he found not only the most meticulous care and medical attention, but also old and new friends. He needed to be among people who loved his poetry. Some of his admirers were staying at the sanatorium at the time. Among them were the Countess Schwerin and her daughter Gudrun von Uexküll, wife of the biologist Jakob von Uexküll. Following his treatment, Rilke moved to the Castle Friedelhausen on the Lahn, the estate of the Countess Schwerin, in the summer of 1905. There, for a time at least, he was spared the worry about his daily existence and gained new stimulations through his association with Jakob von Uexküll. He even seriously considered the study of natural science.

Although he enjoyed the rural existence in Friedelhausen, he was often quite disheartened. Once he wrote about the hours and days in the park and castle, that they "came and went without belonging to us." Rilke felt that he had reached a turning point and that the most difficult part of his life and the most important realization of his inner calling were still to come. The last stanza of his poem "Selbstbild-nis" (Self-Portrait), written in 1906, expresses this mood, fluctuating between doubt and confidence.

> That, barely yet discerned as a connection;
> Not ever tried in pain or in success
> For lasting attainment
> Yet so as if the unconnected things
> Were parts of distant plans.[13]

In the fall of 1905 Auguste Rodin invited Rilke to join him in Paris. When he accepted Rodin's invitation, Rilke did not suspect that Paris was to be his permanent home for years to come. At first Rodin, too, probably thought of Rilke's visit as a short stay, just long enough to give Rilke the opportunity to prepare a new essay on Rodin's work. Out of their talks, which both men seemed to enjoy, a bond slowly developed, a bond that remained undefinable and beset by complications. The underlying cause for the gradual dimming of their friendship is probably to be found in the fact that the well-meaning Rodin made his enthusiastic admirer into his employee. Rilke was to take care of Rodin's daily correspondence, a task for which two hours were set aside every morning. Rilke accepted this post of secretary mainly to be near Rodin, al-

though he by no means scorned the small wage of
two hundred francs per month. Soon, however, he
discovered that worshipful service rendered a genius
is one thing, and a relationship to an employer quite
another. Moreover, the stipulation of two hours was
not adhered to. The work heaped upon him usually
took the entire day. Despite this, his salary remained
the same, although it must be said that Rilke allowed
himself several brief vacations during his six-month
term of employment.

Rilke described himself as a "kind of secretary."
He probably only enjoyed this role when a letter to
a well-known artist was to be written. An example of
this was a letter to the great actress Eleonora Duse,
especially since Rodin allowed Rilke to add his own
admiration for her in a postscript. Less enjoyable for
Rilke were the numerous formal letters of congratula-
tions Rodin sent to his princely clients, for example
to Friedrich August, the not-exactly-artistic last king
of Saxony.

For seven months Rilke lived in a cottage on
Rodin's estate in Meudon-Vat-Fleury. An early riser,
Rodin would get his secretary out of bed at five o'clock
in the morning to take him on extensive morning
walks, sometimes as far as Versailles. For Rodin this
was the best time of day for conversations about his
work and for his contemplation of nature. In the gar-
dens of Versailles and Saint-Cloud, Rilke was to learn
through Rodin what the grandeur and beauty of
France consisted of. But apparently Rilke did not have
the stamina it took to work near Rodin. He was

away quite often—Christmas and New Year's Day of
1905 in Westerwede and Bremen; March 1906 in
Prague, where he visited his dying father; after that
in Germany again. It is a question whether it was
Rilke's trips or his indiscretions—which Rodin re-
sented in his secretary—that were the cause of Rodin's
irritation. In May 1906 an ugly scene took place and
Rodin's anger, long suppressed, erupted. Between one
day and the next, he showed Rilke the door.

He had been thrown out like a thieving valet,
Rilke wrote to his wife, but he never hinted at the
real reason for the break. It is quite possible that
imponderables of French social conventions played a
part, conventions Rilke did not recognize in time. Possibly he mistook politeness for cordiality and forgot
that a foreigner rarely manages to be accepted in the
house and closed circle of a French family. An employer remains an employer even though he may be
Rodin. Rilke did not find patrons in France.

It shows the generosity of Rilke's mind that he
could separate the personal from the objective. When
his second essay appeared in 1907 (it later became
part of his book on Rodin) he did not go back on his
admiration of Rodin. Though slightly more reserved
in tone than the essay of 1902, this essay on Rodin
also became an important literary work. It was not
until several years later that Rilke clearly moved away
from his former hero. In a letter to Lou Andreas-
Salomé he spoke about the seventy-year-old Rodin in
almost devastating terms: "something niggardly, a
sticky pettiness," the letter said, had overcome Rodin

and "made his old age into a grotesque and ridiculous thing."

In art, too, Rilke had turned to new gods: Cézanne and Picasso. If one looks at the small statue the Russian sculptor Prince Troubetzkoi made of the aged Rodin, Rilke's later desertion of his hero becomes understandable. This stocky man, his head held high, his waving beard rippling over his corpulent body, was not the towering figure that was expressed in Rodin's own famous statue of Balzac. Rodin did, however, share some qualities with Balzac—the speculative spirit, the craving for money and prestige.

6

The

Circle

of Patrons

Free of the bothersome secretarial chores, Rilke could once more devote himself to his own work and follow his inclinations. He discovered the city on the Seine all over again. "Paris, the light, the silken one, Paris, that has been faded once and for all from her skies, and to her waters to the heart of her flowers, by the scorching sun of her kings."

One thing Rilke had learned from Rodin—"Only objects speak to me, objects perfect within themselves." He began to write "object poems"—which, to him, were three-dimensional, objective structures. These were to be collected in *Neue Gedichte* (1907; New Poems) and *Der neuen Gedichte anderer Teil* (1908; New Poems, Second Part). With renewed vigor he returned to his novel, *The Notebooks of Malte Laurids Brigge*. Rilke was now able to work relatively free of worries because a patron, the banker Baron Karl von der Heydt, had agreed to give regular financial assistance to him and his family. On several occasions Rilke was the baron's guest at Wacholderhöhe House in Bad Godesheim.

Following the advice of the poet Émile Verhaeren, Rilke visited Verhaeren's homeland, Belgium. In beautiful verse and visual language Rilke invoked the old city of Bruges, "*la ville morte*," in his poem "Quai du Rosaire" (Street of the Rosary). He also visited Furnes, Ypres, and Ghent. This journey was to be "important and beneficial for the coming work period." The question, however, after this productive summer of 1906 was where to spend the winter without pressure. It was a favorable circumstance that friends

60

invited him to Capri. Only now did he enter
unencumbered into the world of antiquity. Of the
"sculpture poems" written during this time, "Der
archaische Torso Apollos" (The Archaic Torso of
Apollo) may well be the most beautiful. Even his
most unforgiving opponent Gottfried Benn later
praised these stanzas, although he disliked Rilke's propensity for the comparative "like."

> And would not break out of all his contours
> Like a star; for there is no place
> That does not see you. You have to change your life.[14]

Did Rilke change his life? At any rate, he constantly demanded change of himself. For him, change
meant to take fresh measure of the world and his
inner world, to affirm it anew. In Capri he lived in
surroundings that seemed unchanged from the days
of classical Greece and Rome:

There is no landscape more Greek, no ocean more vast
with antique expanse, than the landscape and the ocean
I can see and experience on my walks in Anacapri. Here
is Greece, without its art treasures, but almost as it was
before they were created. The rocky slopes are there, as if
everything were still to come, even as if the gods were still
to emerge, the gods who brought forth Greece's abundance
of horror and beauty.

Literary history, which easily leans toward artificial divisions into periods of work and of life, talks
about 1905 to 1910 as Rilke's middle period. The fact
is that these were extremely productive years, full of
intense living and intense work. The *New Poems* were
created in those years. His two requiem poems ap-

peared, flouting all traditions. One was about Paula
Modersohn-Becker, the other about the young poet
Wolf von Kalckreuth. And in these years Rilke wrote
most of *The Notebooks of Malte Laurids Brigge*, which
he had begun in Rome in 1904.

Besides the support of the Baron von der Heydt,
Rilke gained other patrons during this time, who
freed him of the daily struggle for existence. Furthermore, since 1906, the well-funded Insel Verlag had
taken over the publication of Rilke's total work. The
owner of the publishing house, Anton Kippenberg,
even paid Rilke a monthly stipend, irrespective of the
publication or sale of his books.

Rilke's critics, the benevolent as well as the hos-
tile, have repeatedly accused him of having exploited
his patrons' generosity. Even up to the present time
the legend is propagated that Rilke was a recipient
of alms—at times a not even subtle one—who had no
qualms about accepting his friends' hospitality. Those
who think in such terms misjudge the essence of
"patronage," which rests on free consent among
friends. The patron does not buy art and commission
the artist out of selfish needs. The archetype of the
unselfish and idealistic patron of the arts was a Roman
called Maecenas, a friend and adviser of the emperor
Augustus. Maecenas gave no commissions to poets or
artists; he was not even an art collector. He was a
close friend of Horace, with whom he shared his
money freely, although the great Roman poet was not
poor by any means. Maecenas gave Horace sizable
sums of money and other goods to be used at his

pleasure, in the expectation of giving impetus to his friend's poetic inspiration.

There is in reality only one kind of patronage: that born of true friendship; and it is thus equally rare. Many men of outstanding talents, sometimes men of great creativity, have been lonely and have perished, beset by outer and inner distress. If the delicate and easily disconcerted Rainer Maria Rilke had not found patronage, he would undoubtedly have become the victim of the principle of the survival of the fittest. There were almost no state subsidies, and he was not suited for the post of a paid court poet. In any case, to the shy Rilke, institutions of any kind were highly suspect. Perhaps Rilke had a genius for friendship and was not merely one who sang the praises of women. During his time, capitalism was in full bloom, and side by side with the growing wealth emerged a perennial mass poverty. On the fringes of this the non-affluent middle class, from which Rilke sprang, struggled painfully to retain its position.

Rilke's personality—both charming and reserved, and in many ways touching—was well suited to creating the desire to help, especially in people who were attracted by his charisma. It is not true at all that Rilke, though originally poor, courted well-to-do patrons. On the contrary, gently but consistently, to the point of impoliteness, he withdrew from the would-be benefactors who approached him obtrusively.

Rilke did not make it easy for his large community of friends and admirers. It was most difficult for those who wanted to be assured of their own values

through the medium of his poetry or who believed
they would become part of the vanguard by sharing
his supposedly sophisticated tastes. When they realized that the presumed mystic was a man who actually
invoked, alongside the "beautiful," the terror and horror of actual conditions, they called him a "perverted
aesthete."

In those years impressionism finally found a broad
base. Architects, craftsmen, art critics, aesthetic re-
formers of all shades (such as those in the Werkbund,
an association of artists, artisans, and industrialists,
founded in Munich in 1907, whose aim was to make
objects beautiful) prepared the intellectual climate,
which spawned extreme individualism. The impres-
sionistic aesthetics extended from the decadent re-
finement of British dandies (among whom were Oscar
Wilde and Aubrey Beardsley), the Parisian symbolists
and Nabis (a group of artists active about 1890), to
the Viennese secessionists and the circles around
Henry van de Velde and Harry Kessler in Weimar.

The daring images of Rilke's words, appearing
almost snobbish at times—those in the *New Poems*
especially—fascinated the public of the aesthetic
salons.

> In mirror images like Fragonard's
> Their white and rose still offers you
> No more, than one who tells you of his love:
> She was still soft with sleep. . . . [15]

To talk with such playful elegance about the flamingos
of the Jardin des Plantes was a sensation for literary
gourmets.

But Rilke's *New Poems* contained more than poems with aesthetic themes, more than poems with concretely sensual images. Rilke moved more and more away from lyrical mood painting and created, with ever grander designs, a monumental style of his own, in which antiquity, the Bible, the Middle Ages, baroque France, and also nature in its animal and plant forms came to life. Rilke attempted to put order into the diversity of his visions, abandoning himself to the most daring inspirations, comparisons, and trains of thought. The contrasts in this world captured his imagination: the intoxicating and the sobering, the splendid and the repulsive or even loathsome. The titles of the following poems indicate the stark subjects of some of these poems: "Morgue," "Der aussätzige König" (The Leprous King), "Totentanz" (Dance of Death), "Leichenwäsche" (Washing of the Corpse).

In October 1907 Paula Modersohn-Becker died, a few weeks after the birth of her first child. During her last stay in Paris in 1906, Paula had met Rilke once more. She had painted Rilke and had painted him the way *she* saw him, not the way Rilke saw himself. He kept a stubborn silence about this portrait, which was later to become famous. Paula, the expressionist, painted the "inner" picture she beheld: simplifying in great strokes, denying the aesthete, affirming the prophet. It is not surprising that Rilke did not want to recognize this portrait of himself. In his requiem "Für eine Freundin" (For a Friend) he wrote what may be the strangest lament ever written:

I thought you had gone further. It confuses,
That *you* above all others erred, you who have
Brought more change than any other woman.
That we are startled at your death, no,
That your stark death darkly interrupts us,
Tearing the up-to-now away from the since-then
That does concern us, and to fit this in
Will be the work we have to do with everything.[16]

In 1907 Rilke also wrote the poem "Gesang der Frauen an den Dichter" (The Women's Song to the Poet), an imploring invocation that might serve to refute the widespread misconception that Rilke's relationships to the opposite sex were almost always those of a brother or a son.

That which was blood and darkness in the animal
Grew to a soul in us and goes on crying
As a soul. And it cries out for you—
Yet you receive it only with your vision,
As if it were a landscape: tender without lust.[17]

Moreover, Lou Andreas-Salomé had made him aware of the forces of the unconscious, the "blood and darkness," at a time when those insights were not yet common knowledge. As early as 1903 Rilke had written to a young poet (Franz Xaver Kappus), in connection with a sensual love poem by Richard Dehmel, the following lines, affirming Freud's teachings: "And it is true, that the artistic experience comes so unbelievably close to the sexual, its pains and its joys, that the two phenomena are really only different forms of the same longing and bliss."

Thanks to more favorable external circumstances, Rilke was able to develop his creative faculties in a far better ambience than in his first years in Paris.

Beginning with the summer of 1908, he lived in a small apartment in the Palais Biron, with windows facing the park, near the Esplanade des Invalides. Now Rilke could work in light, high-ceilinged rooms with a view over a garden, a round pool in the background, at a large oak table that Rodin had lent him. In such surroundings, Rilke confessed, he found: "joy, confidence, and determination" to perfect his far-reaching literary plans, mainly for his novel, which had repeatedly been interrupted and delayed. He also had finally succeeded in breaking out of his voluntary-involuntary isolation. Besides Verhaeren, he became friendly with the French poet Francis Jammes, and also with the novelist Romain Rolland, who would receive Rilke in his small workroom and play classical music for him on the piano. Rilke's meeting with André Gide, whom he recognized even then as one of the most important French writers, was especially important. He later translated Gide's *Le Retour de l'enfant prodigue* into German.

Slowly, the name Rainer Maria Rilke attained European renown. With this, his social standing rose. Aristocracy, insofar as it had literary pretensions, took note of him. During his stay in Paris, Rilke made the acquaintance of the Princess Marie von Thurn und Taxis, and of the Countess de Noailles, who wrote poetry. Within the widely ramified circle of Rilke's patrons, the princess occupies a unique position. She became one of his most faithful admirers. She owned a castle in Duino on the Adriatic coast, the name of which was to become immortalized in Rilke's *Duineser Elegien* (Duinese Elegies).

Now Rilke had enough leisure to move in society and, invited by friends or on his own, to travel through France and abroad. Only now did he get to know and love the landscape of the Île de France (". . . strong in storms and gentle in the light. . ."). He visited cathedrals and museums, cities and monuments, all the way down to Provence. The south of France spoke more strongly and decisively to him than anything else. The discovery of Cézanne's work may have played a part in this, for Rilke responded to Cézanne's work with understanding and sympathy. Looking at the Roman amphitheater in the small town of Orange, Rilke felt close to the great creations of the Greek tragedians and confessed: "We no longer have a theater, because we have no community." This sentence, like so many other impressions from this very productive period, is to be found in *The Notebooks of Malte Laurids Brigge,* the central point of his work in those years.

It is widespread supposition that *The Notebooks of Malte Laurids Brigge* represents a poetically veiled autobiography. There are things that speak for this theory, and others against. Some passages from Rilke's letters, mainly from those of the first years in Paris, have been incorporated in *The Notebooks of Malte Laurids Brigge* almost verbatim. In his childhood recollections, though, Rilke let himself be carried along by a dreamlike stream of associations. Following the example of Malte, the noble young Dane of ancient lineage, Rilke may have dreamed up a wish of what his own childhood should have been. In this tapestry he wove memories, reflections, aphoristic observations of cultural criticism of his day, and pure dream motifs.

7

The

Monologue

of Malte

Laurids

Brigge

In *The Notebooks of Malte Laurids Brigge* (1910) Rilke's most important aim was to account for his own way of life. "He was a poet and hated the vague," Rilke said about his imaginary self. Malte Laurids Brigge is not the Rilke the majority of his readers know and value. Malte is an engaged artist, with a program transcending social and political trends. This program is: "I am learning to see . . . have I said this before? I am learning to see. Yes, I am beginning. It is still difficult. But I must use my time wisely. . . ." Rilke has Malte walk through Paris seeing it through his, Rilke's, eyes. His "seeing" is a long, searching look. Taking stock of what he had seen, he sometimes achieved a psychic realism, a precision of visual observation that can hardly be surpassed even by the magic realists of the graphic arts or by the analytical surrealists.

The Notebooks of Malte Laurids Brigge has no plot in the traditional sense. A young Dane, seemingly a poet, arrives in Paris for a lengthy stay in order to study. For reasons not immediately apparent, he feels lost, even abandoned, and deathly exhausted. The experiences and impressions of his days turn into nightmares. His "notes" in diary form move on two levels. One level is included in the visual impressions of the great city. In it moves the figure of Malte, lonely among the crowds, constantly confronted by their misery. The other story level moves through the action of the novel like a daydream. Memories follow visions of childhood, of being a child. The childhood scenes take place on an estate of Danish nobility, using figures long since dead: a domineering patriarch of the old type; the lovely dream figure of Abelone.

In sudden changes, as if on a revolving stage, the reader is shown both worlds: the dim, unreal world of the old manorhouse and its feudal inhabitants, and in glaring contrast the unrelenting realism of the city street scenes. Only a diagnostician of horror, almost devoid of pity, could paint this picture of the walls of a rotting tenement:

. . . and from these walls that had been blue, green, and yellow, that were framed by the cracks of demolished partitions, the air of these lives exuded. The clammy, sluggish, foul air, which no wind had yet blown away. Here were the illnesses, the exhaled breaths and the year-old stale smoke. The sweat that drenches the armpits and makes clothes heavy, the staleness out of mouths, and the sour fermenting smell of feet. Here hung the acid stench of urine, and the burning soot, and the gray haze of boiled potatoes, and the heavy smooth smell of grease turning rancid. The sweet, lingering smell of neglected infants was present and the smell of fear of children going to school, and the oppressive closeness from the beds of adolescent boys. Much had been added that had come from below, vaporized from the canyons of the streets, and something more had seeped down with the rain, which is never clean above a city.

The Notebooks of Malte Laurids Brigge is a book of unanswered questions, questions about God, about love, about death. These are the central themes of Rilke's prose work, shaping its character and appearing here in a form almost more confessional than in the poems. About Abelone, Malte's dream love, Rilke says that she "did not turn the intensity of her passion

toward God." She did not want to be loved. Rilke
claims the same thing to be true for the biblical figure
of the prodigal son, whose parable, in an altered version, concludes *The Notebooks of Malte Laurids
Brigge*. What is true for the biblical figure may also be
true for the tale of Malte Laurids Brigge. It is the
story of a human being who does not want to be loved.
On the margin of the manuscript of *The Notebooks of
Malte Laurids Brigge* Rilke wrote: "To be loved
means being burned up. To love means to shine bright
with inexhaustible oil. To be loved is to fade away. To
love is above that."

Rilke's greatest prose work has often been compared with the works of Proust, Joyce, and Kafka.
Such comparisons hold true to only a very limited
extent. True, *The Notebooks of Malte Laurids Brigge*
contains the early forms of interior monologue. Rilke's
storytelling art represents a transitional stage. The passages dealing with Malte's childhood often convey
the graciously tired, bored tone of the *fin de siècle*, the
morbid decadence of Jacobsen and his Scandinavian
successors. The Paris of the *Notebooks*, however, is
imbued with the poisonous breath of the *poètes
maudits* (the depraved poets). Baudelaire's influence
is felt—as is much else that is French.

Rilke loved the French tapestries of the late
Gothic period. Still, the texture of *The Notebooks of
Malte Laurids Brigge* is modern, though it contains
some old motifs.

In 1907, André Gide published his prose poem
Le Retour de l'enfant prodigue. Although this poem
has a very different instrumentation from the para-

phrase of the biblical parable that Rilke was to use to end *The Notebooks of Malte Laurids Brigge*, a related leitmotiv runs through both works. The younger brother of the prodigal son, a third son whom Gide added, leaves, and will not return. Gide's words "Without me, you will be braver . . ." (stated by the older brother) may have attracted Rilke as a counterpoint to his own interpretation of the parable. In his translation of *Le Retour de l'enfant prodigue* into German, Rilke carried the crystalline tone of the French into his own language: into a soft German. The translation became a poetic Rilke creation.

Rilke expressed his views about French contemporary poetry only casually. Of the poets, Baudelaire stimulated him. In *The Notebooks of Malte Laurids Brigge* he quotes Baudelaire's "La Charogne." Here, Rilke believed he had found the objective expression —the "pitiless force"—he believed he saw in Cézanne's work. It was characteristic of Rilke's view of poetic language as visual that he regarded Cézanne as a primary model to be followed, and that he asked himself to realize a development that would parallel the immense progress in Cézanne's paintings.

Several times Cézanne's work directly inspired Rilke poems. One example is "Die Entführung" (Abduction). Rilke was also influenced by other impressionists, by their joy in the sensuous and their luxuriant use of light. In a letter to Kippenberg, his publisher, Rilke made a point of saying how happy the French visual arts made him feel and how strongly they inspired him to fruitful work.

The two requiem poems created in this period of

elation were successful sublimations of his deep anxi-
eties, which were latent in him even at times of
greatest joy. Just as Goethe probably freed himself of
some death wish by writing *The Sorrows of Young
Werther*, so did Rilke—especially in his requiem for
the young Count Wolf Kalckreuth, who had committed suicide—rid himself of the temptation to give
in to the moods of hopelessness. At the end of the
requiem for Wolf Kalckreuth is a line that Gottfried
Benn once said his generation could never forget:
"who speaks of victories? What counts is to survive."

As I pointed out previously, Rilke met for the
first time the Princess Marie von Thurn und Taxis in
Paris in the late fall of 1909. In her *Memories of
Rainer Maria Rilke* the princess notes:

The poet, very punctual, appeared on Monday, December
3, 1909. I was pleasantly surprised, but at the same time
slightly disappointed because I had pictured him so very
differently. Not this very young person, who looked almost
like a child. At first sight I found him very ugly, but at
the same time very likable, very bashful, but with excellent
manners and a rare nobility. He had just finished *The
Notebooks of Malte Laurids Brigge* and he talked about
it, and this seemed strange to me, as if he were talking
about a living being, not about a book. He was still quite
filled with it. "I think in this book I have said everything,
there is nothing left for me to say, nothing . . . ," he
repeated sorrowfully.

It was due largely to the generous hospitality
of Marie von Thurn und Taxis that the next years,
until the outbreak of World War I, were by far Rilke's
most enjoyable years. Rilke found himself accepted as

an equal in circles where his self-stylization met with an appropriate response. Rilke's patroness was born Princess Hohenlohe-Waldenburg, the daughter of an Italian princess. Up to the time of his death, she remained Rilke's motherly friend and adviser, and one might even say that she was his successful champion at the highest level of society. She surrounded herself almost exclusively with painters and musicians, who stayed as her guests in two castles: one in Lautschin, Bohemia, belonging to her husband, Alexander; and one in Duino near Trieste, which she had inherited. Even before she came to know Rilke, two of her favorite guests were Rudolf Kassner, who had brought Rilke to her attention, and Hugo von Hofmannsthal. The princess was herself a talented painter and writer —she translated Rilke's *Duinese Elegies* into Italian— and in questions of art she proved to be a generous and open-minded judge. Undoubtedly Rainer Maria Rilke, often unsociable, eccentric in his wishes and requests, was her most difficult guest. The princess did everything she could to respect his idiosyncracies and to gratify his desire for solitude.

"Yes, Rilke was a child of God," the princess is supposed to have said shortly before her death in 1934. At which Rudolf Kassner remarked: "A perverse child of God." Such harsh judgment could come only from a friend who was of two minds about Rilke, one who considered Rilke's *Book of Hours* blasphemous.

Kassner, who leaned toward Eastern mysticism, edited Rilke's correspondence with Princess Marie. In his preface, which reflects his ambivalent feelings to-

ward Rilke, he presents a slightly distorted picture of
Rilke's inner life, although he remained respectful.
Kassner does lead one to sympathize with the man
Rilke and his contradictions. In lively terms Kassner
tells of the artistic-minded nobility that assembled at
Castle Duino every year. The princess is supposed to
have seen to it that all her guests paid careful atten-
tion to Rilke's readings.

Here, Rilke read the first of his *Duinese Elegies*
to this illustrious audience. He read, as Kassner remarks, in his "rich and full voice" that, "in contrast to
his boyish narrow body, had nothing immature about
it." At those gatherings of the cream of society at
Castle Duino, Rilke, usually very reserved, is said to
have been a good conversationalist who could laugh
heartily. He spent one winter at Duino by himself, a
solitude he had desired and been granted. He was
taken care of by the servants, with whom Princess
Marie had left exact instructions about making him
comfortable. At Duino, Rilke started his work on the
Duinese Elegies, which he finished only after an inter-
ruption of ten years.

In all those years Princess Marie was his confi-
dante, not his inspiration. Despite her romantic
inclinations, she possessed enough practical sense and
knowledge of human nature to free the often helpless
Rilke from some of his unrealistic ideas. He once complained to Princess Marie that the wishes and com-
plaints with which his female acquaintances burdened
him were often beyond his capacity for empathy.
Princess Marie answered him brusquely: "Why should

you constantly want to save these silly geese who
ought to save themselves?" Or, "the devil take them,
he is sure to bring them back."

Between 1910 and 1914 Rilke traveled extensively. Emulating the example of Petrarch, he tried to
gain distance from himself by traveling distances, over
mountains and seas. In November 1910 he accepted
an invitation to North Africa. His journey took him to
Algiers, Biskra, El Cantara, Carthage, Tunis, and El
Kaironan. He visited mosques and saw oases. The
world of Islam appeared to him to be simpler and
more lively than the Christian world. In January 1911
he set out from Naples to visit Egypt. He saw Cairo
and Memphis, Luxor and Karnak, the ruins of Thebes.
But it soon became apparent that the fatigue brought
on by such a trip was beyond his physical strength. He
became seriously ill and found hospitality in the house
of the Dutch Baron Knoop in Helwan, where he
slowly recovered.

The profusion of impressions gained during his
African journey did more to depress and confuse
Rilke than to free and enrich him. He wrote in one of
his letters: "The manifold, the immense, which
spread out before my eyes, around me, beside me,
lives upon lives, has impressed me. But whether some
of it will have enriched me, can only be seen much,
much later."

In June 1911, back in Paris, Count Harry Kessler
took Rilke to see the foremost dancer of that time,
Nijinsky. Rilke felt that after this meeting he should
do something for Nijinsky: "a poem that one can swal-

low, so to speak, and then dance it." He did not get to
it. A prose poem written as a ballet subject did, however, materialize, "Judiths Rückkehr" (Judith's Return).

During the last two years before the outbreak of
World War I, Rilke traveled most of the time. His
restlessness took him to Spain, Alsace, the Black For-
est, Munich, and repeatedly to Italy. He again visited
Assisi, the city of Saint Francis, and his beloved
Venice, which was not too far from the Castle Duino.
Like many other poets and artists, he could not resist
the magic of the lagoon city. This attraction is re-
vealed in the poem "Spätherbst in Venedig" (Late
Autumn in Venice). Inspired by the Venice of the
Renaissance period is the poem "Die Courtisane"
(The Courtesan), in which Rilke personifies Venice.
Another time he talks about the historical realities of
this unique city, calling it "the wide awake, overly
brittle, not at all dreamed of: the Venice that has been
willed in the midst of nothing onto sunken woods,
Venice that is all there."

A long trip through Spain followed in 1912 and
1913. Rilke stayed in Toledo, Córdoba, Seville, Ronda,
and Madrid. In Toledo he gazed for a long time at El
Greco's paintings, and they strengthened his inclina-
tion to paint with words. As if with El Greco's eyes,
he saw the famous view of Toledo.

Much that Rilke saw in Spain aroused his opposition. In his remarks on his journey he flew in the face
of traditional ideas, as when he remarked that the
great mosque in Córdoba had been disfigured by

turning it into a cathedral in the Middle Ages. The eradication of the Islamic culture incensed him. After Córdoba, he confessed to an almost violent anti-Christian sentiment. He made fun of the Christian tourists, especially the Americans, who "over and over again make a brew from tea that has already steeped for two thousand years."

Rilke's religious feelings in his daily life were manifested by his identification with all living things, down to the "ugly little bitch" in Ronda that begged for sugar at his table. Of this seemingly banal occurrence he wrote: "We read Mass together, so to speak; the action itself was nothing but giving and accepting, but the meaning and the seriousness, and the entire communication between us, knew no bounds."

After he returned from these trips, Rilke realized that he would soon have to leave Paris. Personal entanglements may have been the decisive factor in his decision to leave. He was as little suited for the role of a social lion—a role into which his admirers would have liked to push him—as he was for the role of that irritable, fickle lover into which his own impulsive behavior and that of others sometimes pushed him. Paris, which had for a time been the point at which all directions and human tensions converged, again became a "place of damnation," as he wrote in December 1913. Longing for Germany overwhelmed him. For the first time he turned to the treasures of German intellectual life and art, above all to the works of the romantics. Following the advice of friends, he again traveled in Germany. He rested in the Black Forest. While there

he visited Kolmar (then still German), in which he
saw the Isenheim Altar of Matthias Grünewald.
Goethe and Hölderlin, whom he had barely read up
to that time, had at last appeared on his horizon.

8

A European between the Front Lines

In July 1914 Rilke left Paris without suspecting that he was not to see Paris for a long time to come. The outbreak of World War I caught him in Germany. This seems surprising, since he had long been aware that trouble was looming. Without actually taking sides on political events, Rilke had voiced his concern and his fear repeatedly during the years before 1914. This can be seen in his remarks about the Russo-Japanese war of 1904–1905 and the war in the Balkans in 1912.

Notwithstanding his esoteric way of thinking, the tremendous upheaval of the era did not pass him by without leaving its imprint. Later literary historians have claimed that Rilke used the symbolic language of the preindustrial time, even that his entire work represents a rearguard action. It is true that metaphors taken from handicrafts and the primal forms of human life styles constantly reappear in his writings; the pitcher, the rope, the house, the bridge, the rose, etc. Yet on the eve of the outbreak of the war, a move toward a radically new style can be discerned in his poetry. The austerity of his language and the growing boldness of his images are definitely the result of a deeply moving experience, which also was revealed in his changed relationship to the graphic arts. Rilke valued Picasso in his role as an innovator, much as he valued the dreamer Paul Klee. On occasion the work of both Picasso and Klee inspired him. *The Duinese Elegies*, Rilke's most important poetic work, is not unaffected by the great movements of that time. His mentor for the new developments and upheavals, most of all for the consequences of the new discoveries in depth psychology, was again Lou Andreas-Salomé, with whom Rilke had again become friendly at the eve of the war.

It would be outside the scope of this work to add new interpretations to the already numerous commentaries on the *Elegies*, this "difficult work, so much in danger of being misunderstood" (Robert Musil). Ernst Zinn, editor of Rilke's collected works, has undertaken the task of working out a chronology for the writer of the *Elegies*. He allots the work of the ten-year period as follows:

In January 1912, in Duino, Rilke wrote the "First Elegy," the "Second Elegy," and notes for the "Third Elegy" and "Tenth Elegy." He also wrote the first lines of the finale of the "Tenth Elegy," which he planned would be the last one.

In November and December of 1912 in Paris and in the spring of 1914 in Paris, Rilke wrote most of the "Sixth Elegy." He also wrote forty-six stanzas that he later decided not to include.

In November 1914 in Munich, Rilke wrote the "Fourth Elegy."

In the fall of 1918 in Munich, Rilke joined all the *Elegies* into a still fragmentary "whole," "in the face of all the uncertainty and danger."

Then in one week of gigantic effort—February 7 to February 14, 1922—in the Muzot Castle, he wrote the "Eighth Elegy" and the "Ninth Elegy," completed the finale to the "Tenth Elegy," and created the last elegy to leave his pen, the "Fifth Elegy," the so-called

"Saltimbanques" (the poem of the acrobats). The work
started in 1910 was not finished.

In February of 1922 Rilke wrote the *Sonnets to
Orpheus*. The fluctuation of Rilke's creativity is unusual in a poet of such stature. Periods of heightened
inventiveness would be followed by long intervals of
fatigue, when his creativity found expression mainly
in letters and in fragments. Still, he tirelessly devoted
himself to revision, to sketches, studies, and reworking
his notes.

During the years of war and civil war, while em-
pires crumbled, monarchs were dethroned, and rev-
olutionaries were the moving forces in the world,
Rilke submitted himself to voluntary isolation, interrupted only by correspondence, and allowed his genius
to mature. A horrified and suffering spectator, he
found no voice with which to protest. When he complained, it was least of all about his own misfortune,
which was that he was temporarily forced into a uniform. For six months in 1916 he was assigned to the
Bureau of War Archives in Vienna. After his discharge
(Princess Marie had used her influence to shorten his
months of woe) he continued his nomadic life—in
hotel rooms, in furnished apartments, often as the
guest of his old patrons.

"If drinking is bitter, turn to wine," the twenty-
ninth sonnet of the *Sonnets to Orpheus* says somewhat
mysteriously. This could have been the motto for the
oppressive war years.

"To be here is beautiful"—there is no question
about those words in the *Elegies*. Still, this often mys-

terious poetry is no secret code of magical incanta-
tions. Rilke felt himself to be neither prophet nor
evangelist. He resolutely refused to explain his
Elegies in Christian terms, or in any religious terms at
all. In January 1923 he wrote that he was moving
away from Christianity ever more passionately. Since
writing *The Notebooks of Malte Laurids Brigge*, he
had made no attempt to search for a newer, deeper
definition of the concept of God. For the writer of
the *Notebooks*, God was one aspect of love, not its
object—a thought obviously born under the influence
of Kierkegaard.

In the *Elegies* there is no revealed God of Christianity, and the old gods are called upon only a few
times. But angels do appear in the *Elegies*—no less
than seventeen times. Counting items alone are cer-
tainly not suited to revealing the contents of a poetic
work; but the frequency with which certain metaphors
and figures of speech occur do point to the themes
in it. What did the figure of the angel mean to Rilke?
What is hidden behind this allegorical concept? It is
probably not too far-fetched to assume that Rilke was
aware that the German word for angel—*Engel*—
comes from the Greek word *angelos*, which means
"messenger."

And who are these messengers of the "beautiful"
and the "terrible"? Where do they come from? Are
they genies, mysteriously guiding demigods? Do they
resemble the god with the lowered torch, Death? In
the "Tenth Elegy" Rilke writes: "I may one day sing
praise and glory to the approving angels." The bitter,

desperate irony of critical consciousness is not to be
overlooked. With acid mockery, Rilke paints the fair-
ground of the outside world: "booths for every kind
of curiosity, bark, hawk, and shout. The grown-ups,
though, have something else to see: how money yields
money, anatomically, not for the pleasure alone, the
sex organ of money, all that instructs and makes fer-
tile. . . ." The question remains open: who are the
angels in such a villainous world that the poet rejects?
In this world of circus fairs and of money?

"World, o beloved, will be nowhere but within."
This sentence, with its commitment to the *Weltin-
nenraum*, the "inner world," represents a final renunciation of what we customarily call "world." Side by
side with the strange interpretation of world as a
metaphor of the inner life, Rilke did not want to re-
linquish the often misused, stale cliché "heart" in his
Elegies. "Heartthrob" and "heartbeat" make their way
through the *Elegies*. Was Rilke thinking of his heart
only? He speaks of the "wilderness within him, this
primeval forest." It is said that he was obsessed by his
inner life. Psychologists may say that he was narcissistic or even excessively introverted. But is this not
true of every poet?

If one considers the great accumulation of Rilke's
metaphors, looking solely at the word content of his
poetry, one sees that it hardly differs from the inven-
tory common to traditional lyric poetry. The *Elegies*
contain lovers, night, the dead, faces, mothers, laments, hands, youths, maidens. Less frequently, the
images are from nature: earth, wind, animals, spring,

summer, fruit, current, air. Almost all of Rilke's nouns are German root words. Such names of mythological figures that he did use are, however, borrowed from other languages. Thus, Rilke's creative strength lies less in a rarefied vocabulary than in his unusual metric composition and in the special way he associates words to make pictures, which are often as visual as works of graphic art. The visual even dominates the musical.

However one wishes to interpret the "unspeakable and inexpressible" in the later poems, in the *Elegies*, and in the *Sonnets*, Rilke's words "poems are experiences" are especially true of the *Elegies*. Experiences —those are readable, discernible insights and intuitions that have turned into objects. Life and death, in Rilke's finely tuned self-awareness, are inextricable parts of being: "but to receive this death, this gentle death, so gently even before knowing life, and not be angry, is ineffable."

And always again the angels, the messengers, are cited:

> Angels (one says) often do not know whether they
> Move among the living or the dead. Eternal current
> Sweeping along all ages
> Forever through either realm and sounding above them
> in both.[18]

Thus says the "First Elegy."

There may be only one key to comprehending, or at least divining that which is so difficult to interpret in the two great poetry sequences, the *Elegies* and the *Sonnets*. This key is again and again revealed by

Rilke's letters. As he himself once said, when his poetic creativity fell silent, he poured part of his creative effort into his carefully written letters. Their total number is estimated to be ten thousand.

In addition to translations from other languages, Rilke wrote some minor works. *Das Marienleben* (The Life of the Virgin Mary), published in 1913, is one of these. These poems express such exaggerated womanly tender sentiments that they can only be interpreted as parodies.

Among Rilke's translations, *Portugiesische Briefe* is of special interest. This is a translation of the famous *Lettres Portugaises* (1669), five passionate love letters purported to have been written by Mariana Alcoforado, a Portuguese nun, to a French nobleman. Rilke was probably moved by the destiny of this woman who, even behind convent walls, did not deny the fire of Eros. Rilke translated twenty-four sonnets of Louise Labé from French into German, that is, into *his* German. These works, like Rilke's version of Gide's *Le Retour de l'enfant prodigue*, should actually be considered variations on someone else's themes, rather than translations.

Die weiße Fürstin (The White Princess), created for Eleonora Duse, whom Rilke admired, could only be published after World War I, although it had been written much earlier.

Interrupted only by the episode of his military service in Vienna, Rilke spent the years between 1914 and 1919 in Munich. With the loss of his apartment in Paris went his scant possessions—precious books, manuscripts, and letters, among which were those of Rodin. A substantial number of the items were auctioned off in Paris. André Gide did manage to salvage at least Rilke's manuscripts. But harder for Rilke to bear than any of the other losses the war brought was the separation from the people who were close to him. He was saddened by the death of those friends who were killed in action, especially that of Norbert von Hellingrath, a young Hölderlin scholar. Until the end of the war, Rilke was a "homeless" man, not only metaphorically but literally. The fall of the Hapsburg Empire even left him without a country.

One of the most painful separations the war forced upon Rilke was the one from his French friend Marthe Hennebert, whom he had met in 1911. She was then seventeen and, as Rilke claimed, "an uninhibited child" of the lower classes. He encouraged her to pursue artistic endeavors, and Marthe was able— largely through the help of Princess Marie, whom Rilke had managed to interest in his protégée—to develop her talent at weaving rugs. The relationship to Marthe outlasted the war, and they renewed their friendship when Rilke was in Switzerland. For many of his relationships, maintained mostly through correspondence, his own melancholy remark held true: "What finally ended in such misery for me, began with many, many letters, lighthearted ones, beautiful ones, which tumbled from my heart. . . ."

Rilke, who wrote the "Fünf Gesänge" (Five Cantos) in the charged atmosphere of the first weeks of the war, has been criticized for not sufficiently dis-

associating himself from the mass frenzy. But in contrast to many famous writers who were swept into
writing enthusiastic, patriotic hymns, Rilke held back.
He recorded only what happened around him and
what seemed to him deeply moving. Within a few
months, however, he had resolutely moved away
from that, too. In any case, these songs are really a
literary homage to his fatherland. Still, a dark, hard
tone cannot be overlooked. He thinks of the victims
and talks of the "heavy, hurtful blanket of pain." One
song ends with: "Your own wrongs flare up in terrible
pain, in agonized hearts." As early as November 1914,
Rilke condemned the war in a letter to his friends
Karl and Elisabeth von der Heydt: "Now the war has
become invisible to me, a sorrowful visitation. . . .
There is no wish to create in me, only to have the
soul survive."

He was deeply shaken when he received the
news of the death of Georg Trakl, an Austrian lyrical
poet, who died of an overdose of drugs—it is not
known whether accidentally or deliberately—in a military hospital. In a letter to Ludwig von Ficker, the
publisher of the periodical *Brenner*, Rilke said Trakl
was one of the few with whom he felt a kinship.
Using von Ficker as intermediary, a well-to-do young
Austrian had donated a substantial sum to Rilke and
Trakl at the beginning of the war. The man was
Ludwig Wittgenstein, who in later years earned world
renown as physicist and philosopher and as author of
the *Tractatus logico-philosophicus*.

From the very beginning of the war, Rilke was an

avowed skeptic "so completely noncombatant," as he confessed to his friend Baron Thankmar von Münchhausen, who had been called up as an officer. He spoke of the war as the "so very saddening doings of humanity in this self-incited misfortune." Rilke could not forget the cosmopolitan city of Paris. In the same letter he said that a Picasso painting, "Les Saltimbanques," hung in his room—a picture "that contains so much of Paris that for moments I forget. . . ."

In the midst of war Rilke condemned the universal slaughter:

Men's own doings, as everything else has been in the last decades, slipshod work, work for profit, except for a few pained voices and pictures, except for a few warning voices, a few spirited crusaders who trusted their own hearts that went against the tide. . . .

Passionately he embraced the idea of peace among nations. In a letter written in September 1917, he wrote:

I sometimes think that every additional day this war goes on the obligation grows for mankind to work for a greater, more benevolent common future, for what could be more of an obligation than the pain, grown beyond all measure, that ought, after all, to draw millions of people in all countries closer together. Then it will be possible to speak again, and every expression of love or art will find a new echo, clearer air, and a wider horizon. I must confess to you, that I want to go on living only to see this come true.

Rilke's belief in a better future, which his friend Lou Andreas-Salomé shared, cemented their friendship anew. Through her he was led to the discoveries of Freud, which had revolutionized the understanding of man. He thanked her for her book *Drei Briefe an einen Knaben* (Three Letters to a Boy), inspired by psychoanalysis, published in 1917. Rilke is extensively quoted in this book, a sensation in its time, which crusades for sensitive sex education. Lou regarded Rilke's idea of "a lifelong womb-relationship of all creatures" as an insight of the nature of depth psychology. Rilke wrote Lou that in spite of all the "chaos, sadness, and distortion," he believed in the "fullness, benevolence, and affection of life."

The revolutionary events of these years moved Rilke and made him feel confident. In November 1918, most of the representatives of a bourgeois humanism—Gerhart Hauptmann, Thomas Mann, Richard Dehmel—were abstaining from political activity. In a letter to Clara, bearing the date of the Munich Revolution, November 7, 1918, Rilke clearly stated his positive feelings about the events. He wrote that he had been busy watching, listening, and hoping: "large assemblies everywhere . . . assemblies of thousands under the skies, and I was one of them." He listened to the speeches of the sociologist Max Weber and those of the "radically anarchistic" Erich Mühsam. With sympathy he noted the appearance of the number of students: "men who fought at the front lines for four years." He carefully followed the speeches of the workers: "all so simple and folksy." At the end of the letter he writes: "that the time is right for taking giant steps. . ."

But, in the face of the renewed strength of reactionary forces, Rilke soon felt disappointed with conditions in Germany. He applied for a Swiss visa. Since there was no longer an Austrian empire, the Prague-born Rilke had to wait quite a long time before he received a passport from the Czechoslovakian republic. As long as his future residence was still uncertain, he remained the guest of Swiss friends. He was never to see Germany nor Czechoslovakia again. This probably caused him little pain, for even during the first years after the war, he was drawn much more strongly toward Paris, where he stayed for a short time in 1919 and found a friendly reception, and Italy. June of 1921 saw him in Venice as the guest of Princess Marie, who wrote in her memoirs: "I could tell that he was still plagued by unrest and indecision."

Finally a refuge that was to his liking offered itself. The industrialist Reinhart, who lived in Winterthur in Switzerland, rented for Rilke's use the small Castle Muzot, where Rilke spent the last years of his life in the castle's tower. The landscape, and the old fortresslike building in the middle of a garden, soothed him. There he finished his *Duinese Elegies*. In addition to the *Elegies* he wrote—in the span of two weeks—the *Sonnets to Orpheus* and "Der Brief des jungen Arbeiters" (The Letter from a Young Workingman). Unlike the *Elegies*, which had progressed painfully and slowly, the *Sonnets* poured from his elated soul almost effortlessly, carried along by rhythm and melody.

Even before the *Sonnets* were created, Rilke had begun again to use rhyme. In 1921 he wrote to Baladine Klossowska, a Russian painter he was friendly with, in Paris: "Say nothing against rhymes . . . the true rhyme is not a mere poetic device, but an infinitely reaffirming yes that the gods deign to afford our most innocent feelings."

Memories of song, music, and dance, the vision of youth and beauty, animate Rilke's *Sonnets*. The *Sonnets* bear the dedication: "Written as an epitaph to Wera Ouckama Knoop." Rilke had met Wera, who was studying dancing, at her mother's house in Munich. In 1919, when she was only nineteen years old, Wera became ill and succumbed to leukemia, the same ailment that was to kill Rilke. Rilke described Wera in his letters as extraordinarily beautiful. She was said to have attracted attention "by the art of motion and measured walking innate to her body and spirit."

The *Sonnets*, in which Rilke used both iambic and trochaic meters, do not actually conform to the traditional concept of the sonnet. In them an old leitmotiv of Rilke's reappears: the conflict between thought and feeling, the alternation between sensual, passionate vitality and poetic, sublime spirituality. Rilke's laments about the world's dissonances, as well as his glorification of the world's joys, are directed to Orpheus, the poet and musician in Greek mythology whose lyre-playing could charm animals and make trees and rocks move.

> A god can do it. But how, pray tell me, shall
> A man go with him through the narrow lyre?
> His mind is discord. At the crossroad of two
> Heart-paths, no temple for Apollo.

> A song, as taught by you, is not desire,
> Not pleading for the finally achieved;
> A song is being. . . .[19]

"The Letter from a Young Workingman," Rilke's last prose piece, is an imaginary letter of twelve printed pages. This letter of homage to Émile Verhaeren is believed to have been written one day after the creation of the "Fifth Elegy," the so-called "Saltimbanques." With this, the letter shares one theme: Paris and the simple people in France.

In the "Fifth Elegy" the image of Picasso's acrobats crowds into Rilke's concept of the workingman of his time:

> The wilted, wrinkled weightlifter,
> The aged, who only drums,
> Shrunk in his wrinkled skin as if
> It had before contained two men, and one
> By now were in the graveyard, and he survived the other.[20]

In contrast to this acrobat is the strong young workingman, who supposedly writes the letter:

Who is this Christ who meddles in everything. Who knew nothing about us, nothing of our work, nothing of our need, nothing of our joy. . . . What does he want of us? They say he wants to help us. True, but he acts strangely helpless when he is near us. His circumstances were so vastly different.

Later, the young workingman writes, sounding almost like a dialectic materialist:

They have made a profession out of Christianity, a bourgeois occupation. They are so overanxious to malign and

cheapen the here and now, which we really should enjoy
and trust, that they hand over the earth more and more
to those who extract a temporal quick advantage from the
misshapen and suspect world, which they deem not worthy
of a better fate anyhow. This increasing exploitation of
life—is it not a consequence of debasing the here and
now through the centuries? What madness to divert us toward a beyond, while here we are surrounded by tasks,
expectations, and the future. What fraud to steal pictures
of earthly joys and sell them to Heaven behind our backs!

The imaginary letter is addressed to Verhaeren.
The correspondent bears many features of Rilke himself, and in his imaginary mistress one can recognize
Rilke's young friend Marthe. Of her, the young working girl, he says: "Her idea of freedom is boundless."
For the girl of the proletariat, God represents the
archpatron, who startles her but no longer frightens
her. Her lover comforts her by saying that there is
"tranquility" in the old churches, and "songs in the
agitated stones."

Like a modern sex rebel, Rilke's workingman
praises the joys of physical love. He reproaches the
narrow-minded powers of the time for repudiating
sexual love, "with that intolerable mixture of con-
tempt, covetousness, and curiosity." He writes:

Here everything is distortion and repression, even though
we owe our being to this deepest of events, and in it we
again possess the essence of our raptures. It becomes in-
creasingly difficult for me to comprehend, if I may say so,
how a doctrine that puts us in the wrong just where every
living creature enjoys his most blissful right, can, with such
persistency, even though standing its test nowhere, still
continue to hold its own.

This long letter, like a prose commentary on his *Sonnets to Orpheus*, ends with an injunction that may well express the mission Rilke felt himself committed to: "Let us have teachers who celebrate the here and now."

In the five years left to him after the completion of the *Duinese Elegies*, Rilke wrote what, compared to his major works, can only be considered incidental work (translations, a number of poems, a poem cycle in French) and letters, always letters, which steadily became less precious. In the place of an often somewhat narcissistic self-portrayal there now appeared a commitment. Rilke conscientiously answered every letter addressed to him. The patience with which he responded to anybody's concern shows the extent of his sympathy, as much in affirmation as in gentle contradiction. The intensely sensitive, ailing man wrote and wrote, often throughout the night, even in the terminal stage of his illness.

Every so often Rilke left the magic circle of his "inner" world and confronted the questions and unsolved problems of his time, even political ones. A prognosis like the following one, about the official German position and the future of Germany may not have been entirely to the liking of some of his aristocratic correspondents, since Rilke's prophecy, written in 1923, also contained his opposition to the reawakening German nationalism.

For me, as I see things and experience them in the only way I can, according to my nature, there is no doubt that it is Germany—in its lack of self-awareness—that holds

back the world. The variegated composition and wide
scope of my upbringing grants me the unique distance to
be aware of this. In 1918, at the moment of collapse, Germany could have shamed and moved everyone, the world,
by an act of deep truthfulness and conversion. Through
a clear and resolute renunciation of its wrongly built pros-
perity, in other words through that humility that would
have been so very much its *real* self and an element of its
dignity that would have forestalled everything, that alien
humiliation could have dictated to it. . . . It wanted to
persevere, not change. And so one feels only: something
remains undone. Something is missing that could have
provided an anchor. A rung is missing on the ladder; therefore the terrible apprehension, the fear, the premonition
of a sudden and violent collapse.

Rilke did not live the life of a hermit in his home
in the Rhone Valley. He left the Castle Muzot several
times for shorter or longer periods—for other parts of
Switzerland to seek treatment and for journeys to Italy
and France. In 1925 he spent six months in Paris,
while his friends—foremost among them the Princess
Marie von Thurn und Taxis—who had gone to Switzerland to visit him waited for him in vain. In Paris he
allowed himself to be honored and praised by his
friends there. No other German writer, not even
Heinrich Heine, had generated that much excitement
in France. The eccentric painter Klossowska helped
Rilke with the preliminary notes to his poems written
in French.

In August 1925 Rilke returned to Muzot, exhausted, literally tired to death. During the last year
of his life he drew even closer to his French friends.
Paul Valéry, some of whose poems Rilke had trans-

lated into German, visited him. The young Maurice Betz translated *The Notebooks of Malte Laurids Brigge* into French. Edmond Jaloux, Charles Du Bos, Charles Vildrac, and Jean Cocteau expressed their admiration of his work. Swiss and German friends made the pilgrimage to Muzot. But the insidious illness sapped Rilke's strength. Very few people knew how seriously ill he was; not even Clara Rilke and Princess Marie knew the facts. Finally, Rilke felt himself compelled to withdraw more and more and to curtail his correspondence.

Rilke had always been intimate with death, a feeling that runs through almost all his poetry, especially the *Duinese Elegies*. Yet, in the last year of his life Rilke did not believe the end to be so near as it was. As late as the fall of 1926 he hoped the southern sun would cure him. But the destination of his last journey was not Italy, for which he longed, but the Val-Mont Sanatorium, above Montreux, where the already dying man was admitted. Only within the last four weeks of his fatal illness did he reconcile himself to his impending death. Physically reduced, he no longer wanted to see anyone, nor be seen. Except for his friend Frau Wunderly-Volkart, who nursed him to the end, and his physician, he allowed no one to see or touch him. Even Clara Rilke was not allowed to see the dying man. Like Niels Lyhne—Jens Peter Jacobsen's hero whom Malte Laurids Brigge so much resembled—Rilke expressly demanded that no priest be called. Like Niels Lyhne, Rainer Maria Rilke died a "hard death."

As an epigraph to Rilke's life and work one might speak these verses from the *Sonnets to Orpheus*:

> Not is the suffering perceived,
> Not ever has love been learned.
> What in death does us snatch
> Unrevealed has remained.
> Only the song overland
> Hallows and honors.[21]

Yet the epitaph Rilke himself chose to be inscribed over his grave in Raron in the Rhone valley is enigmatic:

> Rose, O perfect contradiction, joy,
> To be no one's sleep under so many
> Lids.[22]

Many have tried to decode and interpret these lines, but no one has found the key. The essayist Fritz Usinger has undertaken what may be the most sensitive attempt to interpret this curious epitaph: "Thus, there is a lament hidden behind the poet's statement, a lament about life, which uses the object of sleep, of tiredness, to signify that human strength can last only just so much, the rift between being and demands. This is the poet's great theme of life and suffering."

Rilke, who suffered all his life from the discord and contradiction of life, tried to resolve the dissonances of life with his poetry. Forms of life and art as they had evolved in past cultures should, in his intention, be linked to man's goals for the future.

"Let us have teachers who celebrate the here and now," he has a friend of the young workingman say. Rainer Maria Rilke was such a teacher.

Appendix

1. Ach wehe, meine Mutter reißt mich ein.
   Da hab ich Stein auf Stein zu mir gelegt
   und stand schon wie ein kleines Haus,
   um das sich groß der Tag bewegt,
   sogar allein.
   Nun kommt die Mutter, kommt und reißt mich ein.

2. Des alten lange adligen Geschlechtes
   Feststehendes im Augenbrauenbau
   Im Blicke noch der Kindheit Angst und Blau . . .

3. Traumselige Vigilie.
   Jetzt wallt die Nacht durchs Land;
   der Mond, die weiße Lilie
   blüht auf in ihrer Hand.

4. Alle Mädchen erwarten wen,
   wenn die Bäume in Blüten stehn.
   Wir müssen immer nur nähn und nähn,
   bis uns die Augen brennen. . . .

5. Wer jetzt weint irgendwo in der Welt,
   ohne Grund weint in der Welt,
   weint über mich.

6. Wer jetzt stirbt irgendwo in der Welt,
   ohne Grund stirbt in der Welt,
   sieht mich an.

7. Denn Herr, die großen Städte sind
   verlorene und aufgelöste;
   wie Flucht vor Flammen ist die größte,—
   und ist kein Trost, daß er sie tröste,
   und ihre kleine Zeit verrinnt.

8. O Herr, gib jedem seinen eignen Tod.
   Das Sterben, das aus jenem Leben geht,
   darin er Liebe hatte, Sinn und Not.

9. Denn Armut ist ein großer Glanz aus Innen.

10. Du bist der Arme, du der Mittellose,
    du bist der Stein, der keine Stätte hat,
    du bist der fortgeworfene Leprose,
    der mit der Klapper umgeht vor der Stadt.

11. Sie werden dauern über jedes Ende
    und über Reiche, deren Sinn verrinnt,
    und werden sich wie ausgeruhte Hände
    erheben, wenn die Hände aller Stände
    und aller Völker müde sind.

12. Der Park ist hoch und wie aus einem Haus
    tret ich aus seiner Dämmerung heraus
    in Ebene und Abend. In den Wind,
    denselben Wind, den auch die Wolken fühlen . . .

13. Das, als Zusammenhang erst nur geahnt;
    noch nie im Leiden oder im Gelingen
    zusammengefaßt zu dauerndem Durchdringen,
    doch so, als wäre mit zerstreuten Dingen
    von fern ein Ernstes, Wirkliches geplant.

14. . . . und bräche nicht aus allen seinen Rändern
    aus wie ein Stern: denn da ist keine Stelle,
    die dich nicht sieht. Du mußt dein Leben ändern.

15. In Spiegelbildern wie von Fragonard
    ist doch von ihrem Weiß und ihrer Röte
    nicht mehr geboten, als dir einer böte,
    wenn er von seiner Freundin sagt: sie war
    noch sanft von Schlaf. . . .

16. Ich glaubte dich viel weiter. Mich verwirrt's
    daß *du* gerade irrst und kommst, die mehr
    verwandelt hat als irgendeine Frau.
    Daß wir erschrecken, da du starbst, nein, daß
    dein starker Tod uns dunkel unterbrach,
    das Bisdahin abreißend vom Seither
    das geht uns an, das einzuordnen wird
    die Arbeit sein, die wir mit allem tun.

17. Was Blut und Dunkel war in einem Tier,
    das wuchs in uns zur Seele an und schreit
    als Seele weiter. Und es schreit nach dir—
    du freilich nimmst es nur in dein Gesicht,
    als sei es Landschaft: sanft und ohne Gier.

18. Engel (sagt man) wüßten oft nicht, ob sie unter
    Lebenden gehn oder Toten. Die ewige Strömung
    reißt durch beide Bereiche alle Alter
    immer mit sich und übertönt sie in beiden.

19. Ein Gott vermags. Wie aber, sag mir, soll
    ein Mann ihm folgen durch die schmale Leier?
    Sein Sinn ist Zwiespalt. An der Kreuzung zweier
    Herzwege steht kein Tempel für Apoll.

    Gesang, wie du ihn lehrst, ist nicht Begehr,
    nicht Werbung um ein endlich noch Erreichtes;
    Gesang ist Dasein. . . .

20. Der welke, faltige Stemmer,
    der alte, der nur noch trommelt,
    eingegangen in seiner gewaltigen Haut, als hätte sie
       früher

zwei Männer enthalten, und einer läge
nun schon auf dem Kirchhof, und er überlebte
den andern.

21. Nicht sind die Leiden erkannt,
nicht ist die Liebe gelernt,
und was im Tod uns entfernt,
ist nicht entschleiert.
Einzig das Lied überm Land
heiligt und feiert.

22. Rose oh reiner Wilderspruch,
Lust,
Niemandes Schlaf zu sein
unter soviel
Lidern.

Bibliography

1. Works by Rilke

Leben und Lieder: Bilder und Tagebuchblätter (1894)
Larenopfer (1896)
Jetzt und in der Stunde unseres Absterbens (1896)
Christus, Visionen (1896–98; Eng. tr., Visions of a Christ, 1967)
Traumgekrönt (1897)
Im Frühfrost (1897)
Ohne Gegenwart (1898)
Am Leben hin (1898)
Das Florenzer Tagebuch (1898)
Advent (1898; republished in *Erste Gedichte*, 1913)
Zwei Prager Geschichten (1899)
Mir zur Feier (1899; republished as *Die frühen Gedichte*, 1909)
Vom lieben Gott und Anderes (1900; republished as *Geschichten vom lieben Gott*, 1904 [Eng. tr., Stories of God, 1963])
Die Letzten (1902)
Das tägliche Leben (1902)
Das Buch der Bilder (1902)
Worpswede (1903)

Auguste Rodin (1903)

Das Stundenbuch (1905; in three parts: *Das Buch vom mönchischen Leben, Das Buch von der Pilgerschaft, Von der Armut und vom Tode*; Eng. tr., The Book of Hours: Of the Monastic Life, Of Pilgrimage, Of Poverty and Death, 1961)

Die Weise von Liebe und Tod des Cornets Christoph Rilke (1906; Eng. tr., The Lay of the Love and Death of Cornet Christopher Rilke, 1959)

Auguste Rodin (1907; includes the 1903 essay and a second essay)

Neue Gedichte and *Der neuen Gedichte anderer Teil* (1907 and 1908; Eng. tr., New Poems, 1964)

Requiem (1909)

Die Aufzeichnungen des Malte Laurids Brigge (1910; Eng. tr., The Notebooks of Malte Laurids Brigge, 1949)

Erste Gedichte (1913)

Rückkehr des verlorenen Sohnes (1913; translation of Gide's *Le Retour de l'enfant prodigue*)

Das Marienleben (1913; Eng. tr., The Life of the Virgin Mary, 1947)

Die weiße Fürstin (1920)

Duineser Elegien (1923; Eng. tr., Duinese Elegies, 1930)

Sonette an Orpheus (1923; Eng. tr., Sonnets to Orpheus, 1936)

Vergers suivi des Quatrains Valaisans (1926)

Les Fenêtres: Dix Poèmes (1927)

Les Roses (1927)

Gesammelte Werke (6 vols., 1927)

Erzählungen und Skizzen aus der Frühzeit (1928)

Briefe an A. Rodin (1928)

Verse und Prosa aus dem Nachlaß (1929)

Briefe an einen jungen Dichter (1929; Eng. tr., Letters to a Young Poet, 1954)

Briefe (7 vols., 1929–37; republished in an abridged edition in 2 vols., 1950)

Briefe an eine junge Frau (1930)

Über Gott: Zwei Briefe (1933; includes "Der Brief des jungen Arbeiters")

Späte Gedichte (1934; Eng. tr., Later Poems, 1938)

Briefe an seinen Verleger (1934)

Poèmes français (1935; includes the three earlier collections of poems in French)

Gesammelte Briefe (6 vols., 1936–39)

Tagebücher aus der Frühzeit (1942)

Ewald Tragy (1944; Eng. tr., 1959)

Nachlaß vier Teile (1950)

Die Briefe an Gräfin Sizzo 1921–26 (1950)

Aus dem Nachlaß des Grafen C. W.: Ein Gedichtkreis (1950; Eng. tr., From the Reminiscences of Count C. W., 1952)

Briefwechsel mit Marie v. Thurn und Taxis (1951; Eng. tr., The Letters of R. M. R. and Princess Marie von Thurn und Taxis, 1958)

R. M. R. und L. Andreas-Salomé (1952)

A. Gide: Correspondance 1909–26 (1952)

Briefe an Frau Gudi Nölke (1953; Eng. tr., Letters to Frau Gudi Nölke, 1955)

Gedichte, 1909–26 (1953)

Briefwechsel in Gedichten mit Erika Mitterer (1954; Eng. tr., Correspondence in Verse with Erika Mitterer, 1953)

R. M. R. an Benvenuta (1954; Eng. tr., Letters to Benvenuta, 1954)

R. M. R. et Merline: Correspondance 1920–26 (1954)

R. M. R. und K. Kippenberg (1954)

R. M. R. et A. Gide/ E. Verhaeren: Correspondance inédite (1955)

Sämtliche Werke (1956)

Lettres Milanaises, 1921–26 (1956)

R. M. R. und Inga Junghanss: Briefwechsel (1959)

Briefe an Sidonie Nádherny von Borutin (1969)

2. *English Translations in Collections*

Poems by R. M. R. (1918; enlarged ed., 1943)
The Journal of My Other Self (1930)
Requiem, and Other Poems (1935)
Translations from the Poetry of R. M. R. (1938)
Wartime Letters of R. M. R., 1914–21 (1940)
Fifty Selected Poems (bilingual ed., 1940)
Primal Sound, and Other Prose Pieces (1943)
Letters (2 vols., 1945–48)
Thirty-one Poems by R. M. R. (1946)
Selected Letters of R. M. R., 1902–26 (1946)
Five Prose Pieces (1947)
R. M. R.: His Last Friendship (1952)
Selected Works (1954 ff.)
Poems 1906–26 (1957)
Selected Works: Prose and Poetry (2 vols., 1960)

3. *Works about Rilke*

Andreas-Salomé, Lou. *Memoirs.* Edited by Ernst Pfeifer. 1952.

Batterby, K. A. *Rilke and France: A Study in Poetic Development.* 1966.

Hamburger, Käte. *Rainer Maria Rilke.* 1950.

Hartman, Geoffrey H. *Unmediated Vision.* 1966.

Holthusen, Hans Egon. *Der späte Rilke.* 1949.

———. *Rainer Maria Rilke.* 1957.

Kunisch, Hermann. *Rainer Maria Rilke.* 1944.

Mandel, Siegfried. *Rainer Maria Rilke: The Poetic Instinct.* 1966.

Mason, Eudo C. *Rilke, Europe and the English-speaking World.* 1961.

Puknat, E. M., and S. B. "American Literary Encounters with Rilke." In *Monatshefte* 60 (1968):245–56.

Shaw, Priscilla. *Rilke, Valéry and Yeats: The Domain of Self.* 1964.

Wood, F. *Rainer Maria Rilke: The Ring of Forms.* 1958.

Index